AMERICAN CANVAS

An Arts Legacy for Our Communities

WRITTEN BY GARY O. LARSON

NATIONAL ENDOWMENT FOR THE ARTS

TABLE OF CONTENTS

Introduction by the Chairman

Calls to Action

APPENDIX A: American Canvas Forums

APPENDIX B: American Canvas National Committee & Steering Committee

Acknowledgements

INTRODUCTION BY THE CHAIRMAN

One of the joys of being Chairman of the National Endowment for the Arts is experiencing the vast and diverse array of art in America. When I came to the agency in October 1993, I began a canvass of the arts in communities nationwide, and I managed to visit all 50 states, taking the pulse of the arts everywhere. In city after city, the desire for a strong arts presence was manifested in new facilities or burgeoning ideas. The community could be as small as 3,000 or as large as several million; the desire was there, but often, the long-range planning was not. Let's build it, and they will come, and we will worry about tomorrow, tomorrow. This philosophy, coupled with a declining public commitment to funding the arts, was a recipe for disaster.

Some communities did have an infrastructure for sustaining their arts, and while there was no one solution that seemed applicable to all, I felt that rather than reinvent the wheel, we needed to share our ideas and talk about a commitment as a nation to our ongoing arts legacy.

More than 100 years ago, a citizens' movement dedicated itself to preserving and celebrating our natural resources. Out of this was born our national park system and the plethora of environmental groups that exists today. Now, at the end of the 20th century, when America's vision of the arts has had such a profound impact on the world, it seems right to commit to our cultural resources in the same way.

In April 1994, we held "ART-21: Art Reaches into the 21st Century," the first national conference on the arts called by the Federal government. Over 1,000 people came to Chicago to discuss four issues that then loomed large in the non-profit arts: The Artist and Society, Lifelong Learning in the Arts, Arts and Technology, and New Ideas for Federal Arts Funding. Those first steps were interrupted to a degree by the budgetary cuts and restructuring the agency undertook in 1995-96, but the issues remain no less vital. The Endowment, and indeed the entire arts community, began to take a look at the ecology of the arts process, of nurturing the arts and preserving a legacy, and at different models for stabilization and survival. Arts service organizations, such as the National Assembly of State Arts Agencies and the National Assembly of Local Arts Agencies (now Americans for the Arts), the President's Committee on the Arts and Humanities, the American Assembly and a host of others considered the state of the arts in colloquies, conferences and a number of reports.

In 1996, we decided to continue this national discussion by going into a number of communities and meeting not just with the arts leaders, but with representatives of all aspects of civic and social life. The American Canvas, as this initiative came to be called, would be a great vehicle for sharing ideas and information on the issues vital to the nonprofit arts. At each of the American Canvas forums, the structure was designed to take a question for consideration, listen to the responses of all the panelists, and then open it up to the audience.

Each of the six privately-funded forums explored a different aspect of the successful integration of the arts into communities. The host cities were chosen for their leadership in the development of innovative strategies for supporting the arts and using the arts to build strong communities. Each forum began with broad and general questions for the panels' consideration:

1

COLUMBUS, OHIO
1. How can the arts promote civic responsibility and good citizenship? 2. What role do the arts play in community understanding and civic participation? 3. What role do the arts play in cultural heritage and citizen pride?

2

LOS ANGELES, CALIFORNIA

1. How can the arts build and maintain the viability of a community's social infrastructure? 2. How do the arts build a positive legacy for children? 3. What role do the arts play in linking communities and building a solid social framework? 4. How do the arts help to ensure livable communities for tomorrow?

3

SALT LAKE CITY, UTAH

1. How can the arts support education, children, families and communities? 2. How do the arts ensure student success and good schools? 3. In which ways do the arts strengthen family?

4

ROCK HILL, SOUTH CAROLINA ~ CHARLOTTE, NORTH CAROLINA

1. What is the role of the arts in community economic development and growth? 2. How do the arts build communities? 3. What is the Bottom Line? 4. The arts as a community economic resource 5. How can responsibility be taken for America's arts legacy?

5

SAN ANTONIO, TEXAS

1. How can the arts improve the quality of life in America's communities? 2. Why do the arts enrich community life? 3. What advantages do the arts bring to community planning, design and development?

6

MIAMI, FLORIDA

1. How can the arts ensure equity and access to America's culture and heritage? 2. Equity — How do the arts provide opportunities for all citizens and bridge populations? 3. Access — In which ways are the arts available to all Citizens and How do the arts serve the needs of various ccnstituencies? 4. Forms of Expression — How do the arts allow open and responsible exchanges of ideas?

In January, 1997, the American Canvas Steering Committee met to review this dialogue and draft ten Calls to Action. These actions were endorsed on January 30, 1997 by the full American Canvas Committee, a group of national leaders from all sectors of public life. This committee has begun to search for specific ways that their organizations and sectors can work together nationwide to assist communities in ensuring an arts legacy for future generations. A list of the participants and the Calls to Action are included in this book, and summaries of each of the Forums and the participants' responses to the Calls are featured on our World Wide Web site at http://arts.endow.gov under the "American Canvas" section. We see this site as a permanent home for the free exchange of information and ideas on how communities can take action to sustain the arts.

This American Canvas report, however, is primarily an analysis and distillation of the major issues we face in the nonprofit arts. It raises a number of red flags about the current state of the arts in America, and we conclude with challenges and opportunities for everyone in the arts to consider.

The National Endowment for the Arts has undergone radical changes in the past four years, and I am certain that change is the only sure bet for the future. The nature of the public funding network for the arts for the next century depends upon the political will of Congress and state and local elected officials. The very real hope for the arts is that they will be vital in the daily life of communities, and that through the Endowment, communities will, in turn, find ways to sustain the arts at the local level. As a nation, however, we are obliged to take stock of our cultural resources and the quality of life the arts bring to all our citizens. The future of the arts in America depends upon the will of the people. The spirit to grow is there, but a flower can be crushed with a single step. Given half a chance, art will flourish and carpet the landscape with color and life. Let us tend these seeds we have sown and hand down undiminished to our children the artistic legacy we have nurtured.

Jane Alexander

IMPROVING THE CLIMATE FOR CULTURE

"The World leadership which has come to the United States cannot rest solely upon superior power, wealth, and technology, but must be solidly founded upon worldwide respect and admiration for the Nation's high qualities as a leader in the realm of ideas and of the spirit."— NATIONAL FOUNDATION ON THE ARTS AND HUMANITIES ACT OF 1965

How do we measure the health of the arts? Economic data are available, but, as with all economic indicators, are subject to wide dispute. Leading cultural indicators simply do not exist, and the hodgepodge of measurables that are available— sales figures for books and recordings, Nielsen and Arbitron ratings, box-office receipts for theater admissions and the like—raise as many questions as they purport to answer.

Invariably, matters of taste come into play in these discussions, along with distinctions between the nonprofit arts and the entertainment industry, between "high" and "low" culture, between allegedly "uplifting" pursuits and seemingly "mindless" diversions. Because most of us have passionate opinions concerning the art we enjoy, assessments of the current state of American culture are particularly risky, and consensus, unlikely.

What we should be striving for as a nation seems much clearer—in conception, at least, if not in attainment. Congress in the Arts and Humanities Act, which created the National Endowment for the Arts and the National Endowment for the Humanities, stated:

> *The practice of art and the study of the humanities require constant dedication and devotion. While no government can call a great artist or scholar into existence, it is necessary and appropriate for the Federal Government to help create and sustain not only a climate encouraging freedom of thought, imagination, and inquiry but also the material conditions facilitating the release of this creative talent.*[1]

Regardless of one's feelings about public arts patronage, few would dispute the importance of fostering a *climate* conducive to the creation, presentation, and enjoyment of art. Even as the pendulum swings inexorably in the direction of smaller government, there is general acceptance of the importance of the arts to American life. Few would disagree, certainly, with James Michener's recent "open letter" to elected officials in *This Noble Land: My Vision for America* : "…Whatever you do," the popular novelist advises, "encourage the public to support art programs in schools, facilitate art festivals in the countryside, and establish the image of a nation that loves and respects the arts, for that is one of the hallmarks of a first-rate civilization."[2]

The best means of achieving those hallmarks are not nearly so apparent. Nor, unfortunately, are we apt to spend a lot of time pondering such questions. Our cultural climate receives nowhere near the attention that the meteorological climate does. Flaws in the "aesthetic environment," (aside from occasional attacks on the real and imagined excesses of popular culture), are much less likely to make the evening news than problems in the natural environment.

Remarkably, ever since the *Saturday Review* gradually faded from the scene in the mid-1970s, the country has lacked a major, national publication devoted to the arts.[3] Niche-market journals cover the various disciplines quite effectively (but none with a readership anywhere near the top 100 general circulation periodicals,

---

[1] USC 20, ch. 26, subch. 1, sec. 951 (2) (7).

[2] James A. Michener, *This Noble Land: My Vision for America* (New York: Random House, 1996) 203.

[3] Diana A. Chlebek, "*Saturday Review*," in American Mass Market Magazines, ed. Alan Nourie and Barbara Nourie (New York: Greenwood Press, 1990) 457.

however), while the major news weeklies give scant, often superficial, coverage to the arts. Commercial television long ago abandoned even a pretense of serving the arts comprehensively, and while there are more news programs on television than ever before (or programs masquerading as news), the closest thing to cultural affairs programming is the promotional fare of *Entertainment Tonight.* On cable, neither the Arts and Entertainment Network nor the Bravo Channel, which relies heavily on British imports, provides a regular forum for living artists. Nor do they attempt to address contemporary issues in the arts. Public television has done its part to fill the void, but its three-percent share of the broadcast marketplace severely limits its impact.

Aside from an occasional headline, then, announcing what appears to be a purely isolated problem (with the local theater company announcing a large deficit, the symphony orchestra musicians going out on strike, or the museum cutting back its hours), most Americans are blithely unaware of the conditions of the nonprofit cultural sector, or the extreme financial pressures under which most arts organizations operate. Nor do the problems of the individual artists who make it possible for these organizations to exist at all rate even an occasional headline, with low wages and chronic underemployment all a part of the "hidden subsidy" that helps keep the arts afloat. Such alarms have been sounded in the past, to be sure, most notably in the 1960s with the release of groundbreaking economic studies by the Rockefeller Brothers Fund, *The Performing Arts: Problems and Prospects* (1965), and William Baumol and William Bowen's report for the Twentieth Century Fund, *Performing Arts—The Economic Dilemma* (1966). But after three decades of furrowed brows and stiff upper lips, the nonprofit arts seem destined to live a precarious existence in this country.

Part of the mission of the National Endowment for the Arts is to help improve the material conditions for the cultural climate and to encourage "freedom of thought, imagination, and inquiry." Through its grantmaking and leadership, the Endowment assists nonprofit arts organizations and artists, and through its position as a national convener, the agency strives to bring these issues to greater public attention.

The American Canvas initiative attempted to focus on the challenges that must be overcome if the cultural climate is to improve. Over the course of a year-long series of meetings in communities as diverse as Los Angeles, Columbus, Salt Lake City, Miami, San Antonio, and Charlotte/Rock Hill, more than 150 panelists convened, representing a broad spectrum of interests, from business and education to social services and civic affairs (see Appendices A&B for a list of participants). They informed this report and helped frame the course of action for improving the climate for culture in the 21st century. By its very nature, a dialogue with hundreds of participants is fragmentary and disjointed, but certain ideas and concerns rose to the top in city after city. Together with our own research and additional dialogue in town meetings these past four years with arts and civic leaders from around the country, this report is the next step in the dialogue and outlines our central concerns and recommendations for moving forward.

TRANSMITTING OUR CULTURAL LEGACY. What kind of cultural legacy will we leave behind? How inclusive will it be? How varied in form and substance? Will our children be prepared, in any case, to appreciate that legacy? Can we afford to entrust this task to the ever-more-dominant commercial sector, which, however impressive its profits, tends to regard its products as interchangeable, ultimately disposable parts of popular entertainment?

Cultural legacy, in short, a term that invites the kind of ceremonial prose normally reserved for solemn occasions, presents real problems that won't be solved by mere heartfelt sentiments and lofty intentions alone. Rather, the process of retaining key elements of our culture and ensuring their safe passage into the future demands a more rigorous examination of the existing climate for the arts, and of the conditions in which artists and arts organizations are forced to operate today. Some art forms lend themselves more readily to preservation than others, some lack the institutional clout and access to capital that such preservation requires, while still other forms of expression, the subject of contention and debate today, are anything but assured of a receptive audience in the future.

As surrounded as we are by myriad forms of arts and entertainment, the number of strikingly original American voices that find themselves so far from the cultural mainstream as to be virtually silent—in music and literature especially, where popular forms of the mass media threaten to overwhelm all others—is staggering. At the heart of these contradictions, as John Sullivan, executive director of the Theatre Communications Group pointed out at the final American Canvas meeting in Washington, DC, is the tension that exists between private gain and public responsibility, a tension we've begun to acknowledge in the natural environment, but one that we still tend to gloss over in the aesthetic. We do so, Sullivan suggests, at our peril.

"What all of this is about," he explains, "is driving the not-for-profit culture into the marketplace, so that there are no distinctions, so that all of our ideas

Organizations like the Delta Blues Education Fund
keep the blues alive through programs and
workshops in Mississippi schools.

PHOTO BY REX MILLER

are shaped by the marketplace…We need enclaves where ideas are not driven by capital, we need not-for-profit enclaves where ideas emerge for other purposes than the advancement of capital."

THE EVOLVING CULTURAL LANDSCAPE. For better or worse, and probably more than a little of each, the "infrastructure" of the nonprofit arts in America is currently undergoing a number of changes. Not always fully understood even when it works, the system is now straining under shifts in public and private support, increased competition for income, and an aging audience base, all of which raise concerns that cannot be ignored. More encouraging, perhaps, but equally complex, are issues surrounding the identification of new revenue streams for cultural programs, tapping "nonarts" funds in the public sector, or relying on new and closer ties with the commercial interests in the private sector. Not all of these avenues are attractive to an arts community that has enough on its hands merely attempting to stay afloat. But none of these issues can be skirted, particularly since it has become apparent that merely maintaining the status quo is neither desirable nor even possible.

Among the more important lessons of the American Canvas is the recognition that the administrative and fiscal practices that served the nonprofit arts so well during their ascendancy over the past three decades will not necessarily prove as effective in the new century. If nothing else had changed, the sheer increase in the size of the arts community since the establishment of the Arts Endowment in 1965 would have made for a much different, much more competitive environment. And when ever-more-pressing social problems, from AIDS to homelessness to drug abuse to race relations, are factored into the equation, each demanding attention in a context of deficit reduction at the federal level and balanced budgets in many states, it is little wonder that the soaring growth curves that the arts achieved in years past have proved impossible to sustain.

So, too, have the many new opportunities that have arisen in recent years added to the complexity of the cultural landscape. From the belated recognition of America's cultural diversity to breakthroughs in technology, the variety of new options for cultural programming has contributed to the rapidly changing context of the arts in America. The closing years of the 20th century present an opportunity for the reexamination of the structural underpinnings of the nonprofit arts and for speculation on the development of a new support system: *one based less on traditional charitable practices and more on the exchange of goods and services.* American artists and arts organizations can make valuable contributions—from addressing social issues to enhancing education to providing "content" for the new information superhighway—to American society.

As the new century dawns, artists and arts organizations can "make the year 2000 a national celebration of the American spirit in every community," as President Clinton has suggested. But the real challenge, and the reason why a reexamination of the nonprofit arts infrastructure is so important, is an even greater one: to offer an alternative to conglomerate culture, to make those millennial celebrations look less like the half-time show of the Super Bowl, a triumph of American marketing, and more reflective of the true depth and variety of our culture, a triumph of American creativity.

AMERICANS AND THE ARTS. It is also necessary to look at the "demand side" of the equation, to examine the individual and interpersonal implications of our art beyond the institutional inventories and attendance statistics by which we traditionally measure our achievements. Central to the American Canvas process was the need to reassess the varied relationships Americans have with the arts. Many of the panelists, having worked directly with the public in their daily activities, were able to offer a clear sense of the fundamental challenge that confronts the arts community at the close of the 20th century.

Sad to say, many American citizens fail to recognize the direct relevance of art to their lives. The product of an educational system that at best enshrined the arts as the province of elite cultures and at worst ignored the arts altogether, some people understandably view the arts as belonging to someone else. "Most…people," as William Wilson of Brigham Young University expressed it in the Salt Lake City forum, "if you talk to them about art, they're going to say, 'Art belongs out there. That's not part of my life.'" Failing to acknowledge their own expressive activities as part of the full spectrum of the arts, many of these Americans are apt to look with suspicion at an "arts world" that seems alternately intimidating, incomprehensible, expensive, alien, and, thanks to the generally poor job that the mass media have done in covering the arts, often disreputable. "We need to make people aware of how the arts fill their lives if we want their support," suggested glass artist Kate Vogel at the American Canvas forum in Charlotte.

> …I believe it all comes back to the inability of people to view themselves as a part of the arts. Our challenge will be helping people to know us and feel a part of us. We need to take down the barriers. To win over our adversaries we can begin by taking art off the pedestal. It is the feeling of being separate from art that brings the opposition. We must find common ground with those who oppose us, knowing that we won't agree on everything, but there will be some areas where we can work together.

The American Canvas forums uncovered a vast reservoir of strong conviction concerning the integral role that the arts can play in the lives of all Americans. Realistically, not all of the themes to be addressed in this context are positive, but even the less fortunate trends—the tendency for publicly supported art to find itself embroiled in controversy, for example, or the inability of many younger Americans to see beyond the dominant popular culture that literally engulfs them—can be used to the arts' advantage. As the American Canvas participants made clear, the arts:

~ Express our values and aspirations, giving voice to beliefs and sentiments that cannot be communicated as effectively in any other language.

~ Reflect our diversity, providing a neutral ground on which Americans can learn more about one another.

~ Bring us together, fostering celebration rather than confrontation and offering a means of exploring what each of us, regardless of background, has in common.

~ Embody family activities and values, lending an element of stability and offering a shared experience to which all members of a family can contribute.

~ Encourage active participation rather than passive observation, an opportunity for self-expression and personal achievement in the face of a popular culture which tends to reduce all expression to a homogenizing common denominator.

The spirit of Creative America has spurred us to say

and write and draw what we think, feel and dream.

. . . to celebrate through dance, in songs, in paint

and on paper, the story of America: of who we are,

where we have been, and what we hope to be.

HILLARY RODHAM CLINTON

CULTURE AND COMMUNITY. Just as the arts loom large in the lives of many individual Americans, so can they exert an equally profound influence on our communities. The sense that art is firmly entrenched at the margins of many American communities is the result of a variety of factors. The arts community itself bears a measure of responsibility for the marginalization of the nonprofit culture. In the course of its justifiable concern with professionalization, institution-building, and experimentation during the 60s and 70s, for example, the arts community neglected those aspects of participation, democratization, and popularization that might have helped sustain the arts when the political climate turned sour.

Some civic leaders view cultural activities as *amenities* engaged solely in aesthetic pursuits, rather than *necessities* to the health of community life.

Fortunately, the American Canvas forums offered an abundance of evidence from both the cultural and civic sectors suggesting that the arts can indeed play a central role in the lives of our communities. The legacy of the future may have a more common, if no less valued, profile. Included will be the art that is woven through the social fabric, that contributes to the quality of life, fosters civic pride and participation, stimulates the economy and attracts tourists, revitalizes neighborhoods and addresses social problems. Great works of the past won't be excluded from this tapestry—the $60 million in revenues generated by the Cezanne exhibition at the Philadelphia Museum of Art last year is evidence of the power of past masters—but the new cloth of culture will be much more of a quilt, joining a vast array of new patterns that range from folk, vernacular, and popular expressions, to social, political, and experimental works.[4]

Some will bewail, no doubt, the alleged lowering of standards that permits these new forms to enter the "inner circle" of culture. Others will look askance at the utilitarian aspects of art—the "culture of therapeutics," as critic Robert Hughes puts it—that is expected to solve social problems, stimulate the economy, improve the young, and otherwise serve the common good. But in 1997, it hardly seems necessary to debate this point. In a perfect world, to be sure, we might expect the arts to justify their claim on the public purse and the private largesse on the basis of their intrinsic worth. Such justification, after all, is more a matter of translation than of transformation, expressing the value of the arts in terms that civic and corporate leaders—and the average citizen, for that matter—can more readily understand. But a Bill T. Jones who addresses social issues in his work is no less a choreographer, nor Henry Louis Gates any less a historian for tending to the present as well as to the past, and all of us, in fact, are the beneficiaries of their extraordinary efforts.

---

[4] The vagaries of cultural statistics will be addressed more fully in chapter 3, but the $60 million figure for the economic impact of the Cezanne exhibition, supplied by the Philadelphia Museum of Art itself, appears to be an uncharacteristically conservative estimate. One study recently claimed that the exhibition generated $17.5 million in admission and sales of peripheral items, and that the city of Philadelphia received another $122.6 million in tourist expenditures. Tom Csaszar, "The Spectacular Blockbuster Supershow: A Phenomenon of Museum Culture," *New Art Examiner* (Dec. 1996-Jan. 1997):25.

ARTS AND EDUCATION. The cultural legacy that is carried into the next century will count for little if the arts audiences and participants of tomorrow—our children and their children—are ill-prepared to receive, understand, and actively share in that legacy. Serious and systematic arts instruction appears to be the exception rather than the rule for most students. Arts education, in fact, appears to be as imperiled as the arts institutions that need new audiences. Thus along with gaining an overview of the current state of arts education, it is useful as well to rehearse the basic arguments that will prove crucial in seeing that the arts are included in the more general curricular reform movement directed at the graduating classes of the next century. Among those key arguments, according to participants in the American Canvas forums, are the following:

~ The arts are important as a subject in themselves.

~ The arts enhance the study of other areas of the basic curriculum.

~ The arts are relevant to the acquisition of vocational skills.

~ The arts contribute to family unity and growth.

~ The arts offer skills that will be useful as we move further into the Information Age.

~ The arts serve those with special needs, including those who are in danger of falling through the cracks of our educational system.

Here again, the act of translating the value of the arts is called into play, and purists will complain about the ground that is given up in this struggle to wedge a modicum of art instruction into an already crowded K-12 curriculum. But in this area, at least, the issue seems even clearer, and the stakes even higher: to make certain that the arts, in the face of a back-to-basics juggernaut that seems bent on reducing education to a list of academic essentials and dispensable extras, do not wind up in the latter column.

THE ARTS AND TELECOMMUNICATIONS. Few developments in recent memory have received as much fanfare—or raised as many eyebrows—as the Information Superhighway. The last thing the arts community in America needs right now, surely, is another set of problems to deal with, and without question the moving target that is the Internet represents another set of problems. Nevertheless, the convergence of once-independent sectors that is now underway on the digital frontier suggests a new world that the nonprofit arts cannot afford to ignore. As broadcasters and cable operators, telephone companies and publishers, hardware and software manufacturers, and other commercial interests close ranks in their efforts to determine how Americans will one day receive their news, entertainment, and personal communications, the nonprofit sector must also make clear what it can offer to—and what it has a right to expect from—a system that will almost certainly be commercially driven.

The implications of the emerging telecommunications system, both as a means of reaching the public and as a potential new arts delivery system, will figure largely in the cultural climate of the next century. But while the headlines proclaim a new digital era in which everyone will have access to everything, the fine print is much more cautious, suggesting that the new delivery platform of the 21st century may ultimately prove as hospitable to the nonprofit arts as cable television and commercial broadcasting proved to be in the 20th—which is to say not very hospitable at all.

Having examined these five areas, the "philosophical underpinnings" of our cultural climate today, and doubtless raising many more questions than it answers in the process, this report will turn to more practical considerations, touching first on some of the new approaches that are already underway in the arts community. There are many examples that might be cited, responses to the new conditions, new problems, and new opportunities facing the nonprofit sector, by artists and arts organizations across the country. A few of these will be highlighted here, but the vast majority will necessarily spill over into other forums, including the Endowment's own Web site (arts.endow.gov). These examples, in any case, represent what the leaders of the arts community are already doing to meet the challenge that President Clinton issued in his most recent State of the Union Address:

I'd like to make one last point about our national community. Our economy is measured in numbers and statistics. And it's very important. But the enduring worth of our nation lies in our shared values and our soaring spirit. So instead of cutting back on our modest efforts to support the arts and humanities, I believe we should stand by them and challenge our artists, musicians, and writers—challenge our museums, libraries, and theaters. We should challenge all Americans in the arts and humanities to join with their fellow citizens to make the year 2000 a national celebration of the American spirit in every community, a celebration of our common culture in the century that is past and in the…new millennium so that we can remain the world's beacon not only of liberty but of creativity long after the fireworks have faded.

While the arts community welcomes such a challenge, the task of celebrating the American spirit, of ensuring the safe passage of our cultural legacy into an uncertain future, demands the active participation of many others as well. Thus this report, in the spirit of the "Calls to Action" that the American Canvas committee issued on 30 January 1997 (see Chapter 9: The Challenge to Act), includes a series of challenges of its own, directed at civic leaders, the corporate sector, the entertainment industry, the mass media, parents, and individual citizens alike, and designed to build on the efforts that the arts community has already begun.

Jazz legend Lionel Hampton is presented the National Medal of Arts by President and Mrs. Clinton. These awards recognize the contributions to our nation by master American artists.

Lula Washington, a choreographer and dancer active in working with young people in Los Angeles when she is not on tour, spoke at the American Canvas. "We come together, we have a wonderful conversation. It gets put in a book. We go away. It gets on a shelf or on a videotape and there it sits. So what? We are still where we left off at. We have to be more active," she insisted, aiming her advice squarely at the artists, administrators, and audience members in attendance, but with pertinence for the entire arts community. "We have to be more vocal…Everybody here's got to be charged to do that. I mean, we cannot stop here."

TRANSMITTING OUR CULTURAL LEGACY

"In the long history of man," President Johnson declared at the bill-signing ceremony for the National Foundation on the Arts and Humanities Act of 1965, "countless empires and nations have come and gone. Those which created no lasting works of art are reduced today to short footnotes in history's catalog. Art is a nation's most precious heritage, for it is in our works of art that we reveal to ourselves, and to others, the inner vision which guides us as a Nation. And where there is no vision, the people perish."[1]

Sherri Geldin, executive director of the Wexner Art Center, raised this issue at the initial American Canvas forum in Columbus, and in one form or another it came up at all of the regional meetings. "…The legacy of ancient cultures that remains on the planet today," Geldin observed, "is pretty much only what those cultures created in the way of the arts and architecture and literature and music. . . . Very little that has come down through the ages has not in some way filtered through something that we can all identify as the arts."

[1] *Public Papers of the President, Lyndon B. Johnson, 1965,* 2 vols. (Washington, DC: Government Printing Office, 1966) 1022.

Questions of "legacy" today, admittedly, are apt to turn on more practical considerations, including the size of the federal deficit we'll bequeath to our grand-children, or whether Social Security, Medicare, and other 20th century investments will still be paying dividends in the 21st. And yet it was not without reason that Congress, 25 years after the arts and humanities bill had been signed into law, added the following declaration:

> *To fulfill its educational mission, achieve an orderly continuation of free society, and to provide models of excellence to the American people, the Federal Government must transmit the achievement and values of civilization from the past via the present to the future, and make widely available the greatest achievements of art.*[2]

That conjunction of "past, present, and future" is no mere rhetorical conceit. For it is the peculiar nature of a cultural legacy that all three perspectives are brought into focus at once: an understanding and appreciation of works, beyond the popular expression of the moment, that have withstood the passage of time; a means of presenting that material to contemporary audiences; and a vehicle for preserving and transmitting it, finally, to the audiences of tomorrow.

Overlooking for a moment the difficulties inherent in the first two trans-actions—reaching a consensus on works that warrant preservation, and finding suitable venues to keep them alive and vital—the presumption of future audiences for work that may have struggled for attention in its own time is a hazardous one. The audiences of the next century, the children of today, are currently engaged in a 13-year educational odyssey (the 82 percent fortunate enough to complete that journey, that is), and that process generally gives the arts short shrift.

As audiences for the arts age, and as popular culture becomes ever-more-popular among the very young, the possibility of an unfortunate irony presents itself: even if the greatest works of our time are preserved—everything from the *Concord Sonata* to a Clifford Brown solo, from *Appalachian Spring* to *Angels in America*—what if the audiences of the year 2097 lack the background or the inclination, or even the patience, to come to terms with such works?

---

[2] USC 20, ch. 26, subch. 1, sec. 951 (2) (11).

"Art is not self-evident nor of necessity immediately enjoyable," August Heckscher warned in an essay he wrote for President Eisenhower's Commission on National Goals in 1959. "It requires in the spectator an effort of the spirit and of the mind, sufficient to put himself in harmony with a vision other than his own." Heckscher's contention asks us to align ourselves, for the moment, at least, with the vision of another, is a useful reminder of the shared responsibility that is often over-looked: the audience's obligation to meet the artist half-way, penetrating the social and cultural context from which a given work of art may spring, and of the arts presenter's obligation to assist the audience in making that journey. Not all art is easily grasped, immediately gratifying, or even necessarily pleasant. The satisfaction and sense of fulfillment that result from coming to terms with a work of art and experiencing its resonance in our own lives, is a form of pleasure and intellectual challenge simply unavailable elsewhere.

Merely preserving works of art is no guarantee that our cultural legacy will turn out to be anything more than a time capsule full of curiosities for subsequent generations. How do we ensure the transferral of a cultural legacy to the children of the next millennium?

Two parts of this puzzle will be addressed in later chapters: (1) the arts education that will prepare audiences of the future to appreciate the art of the past; and (2) the nonprofit infrastructure that helps sustain cultural traditions today, independent of the market forces more concerned with promoting new items of entertainment and diversion than with preserving past achievements. However, more remains to be said of the nature of "legacy" itself.

Consider four examples referenced above—Charles Ives, Clifford Brown, Martha Graham, and Tony Kushner—typical of artists that most would agree deserve a place in the cultural legacy of 20th-century America, although they are by no means representative of the full range of American achievement in the arts. They offer merely a hint of contemporary works still to be discovered, of the cultural traditions yet in formation as the make-up of American society itself continues to evolve, and of new forms that are just beginning to emerge from the cauldrons of art and technology. Moreover they represent forms in which authorship is easily assigned, overlooking the countless cultural artifacts and expressions that spring from a collective aesthetic—from the functional to the festive, from basket-weaving and saddle-making to mariachi bands and Balinese gamelans.

Yet the four artists in question are sufficient to raise many of the issues that must be confronted before the transmission of our legacy can be ensured.

COURTESY SEATTLE ART MUSEUM

"A Foothold on the Rocks" by American painter
Jacob Lawrence is part of a series of work around the theme of
African American struggle for equality and recognition.

Visions of the cream rising to the top, of the best and the brightest of our artists eventually receiving their due and winning both critical and popular acclaim bear little resemblance to the experience of most artists in America. For ours is a country that often values celebrity over substance, and is often none too kind to its celebrities either. The genuine artistry of celebrities like a Pavoratti or Meryl Streep is widely acknowledged, and the public reveres movie and popular stars, but as quickly as status and celebrity may be attained, it can just as quickly disappear.

"ARE WE THE DINOSAURS?"

Charles Ives's *Piano Sonata no. 2* (Concord, Mass., 1840-60), more commonly known as the *Concord Sonata*, is an acknowledged masterpiece, typical of the groundbreaking work in polytonality and rhythmic invention with which the Connecticut composer was fully engaged at the turn of the century. Yet several decades elapsed before the work of this great composer was first performed in public, an extreme but by no means atypical example of what American composers must regularly endure. Ives was 72 when his *Third Symphony* was awarded the Pulitzer Prize in 1947, in fact, as he belatedly received a small measure of the public recognition he deserved. His considerable body of work (well over a hundred orchestral, chamber and choral works, and some 150 songs) would finally stand a much better chance of having a life of its own.[3]

If Ives survives today (with no less than 80 recordings of his works in print, and regular live performances), and if he seems ensured of an audience, however limited, in the next century, what of his contemporary, Carl Ruggles (1876-1971), or artists like Henry Cowell (1897-1965), Harry Partch (1901-1974), and Conlon Nancarrow (1912-), American originals all who followed in his path?[4] And what of the hundreds of composers living today, who labor in near-total obscurity? If they can't get a hearing for their works now, beyond campus recitals, performances in "alternative spaces," and independently produced CDs, what chance do they have to become a part of our legacy?

Joe Celli, veteran "new music" composer, performer, and concert producer, sees a mixed picture in this regard. "What has happened in recent years," he explains, "is a diminution in the number of places and 'spaces' and opportunities for live performance, and an acceleration, actually, of the ability to create recordings specifically for the electronic media. It tends to be a confluence of both the availability of high technology of a very superior quality to what we had just 10 or 15 years ago, and composers feeling much more comfortable producing works in that manner." The contemporary composer, in other words, can now produce their own

---

[3] Vivian Perlis, *Charles Ives Remembered: An Oral History* (New Haven, CT: Yale University Press, 1974) 153.

[4] The existence of a composer's work on recordings is only one measure of endurance, and the availability of these recordings in the marketplace is quite another. Of the composers cited, in addition to some 80 record-ings of Ives's work in print, there are 6 featuring works by Ruggles, 24 by Cowell, and 8 each by Partch and Nancarrow. (As a point of comparison, there are over 40 pages of Mozart recordings listed in the most recent Schwann catalog.) *Schwann Opus 8*, no. 2 (Spring 1997). But heaven help the consumer beyond the big city who wishes to sample the work of these twentieth-century American composers. The largest record store in Washington, DC, for example, offered 25 titles by Ives, none by Ruggles, 2 by Cowell, and 4 each by Partch and Nancarrow. CD Now, the largest purveyor of CDs on the Internet (cdnow.com), provided a useful list of works in print, but had only 16 Ives, 2 Ruggles, 1 Cowell, 4 Partch, and 4 Nancarrow recordings available for purchase.

works in their own studios, with digital recording and editing software that places much more control in the hands of the creator. These composers are also benefiting from another technological development—electronic cataloging systems, available to retailers nation-wide—that is helping to break the distribution log jam that has long frustrated the vast majority of artists not associated with major record labels. "Even though you're not going to find our discs in most stores," Celli explains, "these stores have the ability now to at least know where to get those discs if some-one comes in to order them."[5]

There would doubtless be a lot more of those orders if the music received more exposure in the media, both print and broadcast, and although eventually the Internet may help in this regard, right now Celli is not optimistic about the prospects for the contemporary artist. He cites the decline of college radio, once the bastion of a free-wheeling aesthetic that found room for all manner of recorded sound, as one example of shrinking opportunities for alternative voices. "What has happened over the last 15 years is that the big record companies have begun to understand the power of college radio," says Celli, "and they have very clearly co-opted this whole medium. There are, certainly, exceptions, but what was previously known as 'new music' or 'alternative music'…has been co-opted by major labels, where it basically means commercial music that hasn't been successful yet. …It's almost difficult for us to even define ourselves any longer, in terms of who we are. …I mean, who are we? Are we the dinosaurs?"

"THE WORD 'JAZZ' HAS BEEN PART OF THE PROBLEM"

Clifford Brown, a black trumpet player who died in 1956 at the age of 25, reflects yet another legacy issue, typical of those artists whose sphere is not the concert hall, the museum, or the university but other less sanctioned arenas. In Brown's case it was the nightclub, but it could have been the church, the community center, or the front porch—wherever people gather to make art. Unable to enter the closed ranks of "classical" artists, nor sufficiently popular to have much of an impact on the commercial marketplace, most jazz, folk, and traditional artists find themselves caught between the two worlds of high art and mass entertainment.

---

[5] Taking matters into their own hands, 14 independent labels, including Celli's own O.O. Discs, have formed a consortium to market their alternative works both on- and off-line. The consortium can be reached at CDeMusic, 116 North Lake Ave., Albany, NY 12206 (www.emf.org/cde_frontdoor.html).

On the surface, at least, such artists fail to measure up to the standards of either realm, falling short of both the rigorous, formal training and technical precision of so-called serious music, and of the mass appeal and box-office clout of truly popular culture. Judged according to their own standards, however—for an expanded cultural legacy does not imply the abandonment of critical standards—the finest examples of these non-mainstream forms clearly distinguish themselves. In ingenuity, improvisatory powers, emotional impact, and the sheer ability to transform often modest raw material into striking aesthetic statements, the best of jazz, folk, and ethnic traditions stand among the finest achievements of American culture.

Clifford Brown is a case in point. By all accounts a brilliant soloist (and a sufficient number of recordings survive to document the trumpeter's genius), Brown's career may have rivaled that of Dizzy Gillespie or Miles Davis had he lived. More likely, though, the trumpeter's orbit would have been constricted to less lofty realms, joining Fats Navarro, Kenny Dorham, Art Farmer, and Booker Little as largely overlooked masters of the instrument, unlikely to claim their rightful place in the cultural legacy. Not until the spectacular rise of Wynton Marsalis, whose triumphs in both jazz and classical music are unprecedented, did the doors of mainstream culture (and the front doors, at that) swing wide open in acceptance of jazz.

Marsalis's recent Pulitzer Prize for *Blood on the Fields* heralds good things to come, certainly, but it is also a reminder of where we were not so long ago. In 1965, the board of the Pulitzer Prize had a similar opportunity to honor one of the masters of jazz, and it balked at the chance. The three-person music jury recommended Duke Ellington for a special citation, in recognition of the "vitality and originality of his total productivity" over the previous four decades. The full board thought otherwise and rejected the recommendation, prompting two of the three music jurors (*The New Yorker*'s Winthrop Sargeant and *Newsday*'s Ronald Eyer) to resign in protest.[6] Ellington, characteristically poised, was as unflappable: "Fate doesn't want me to be too famous too young."[7] Several weeks later, back on the road with his band for a series of one-night stands, Ellington reflected further on the Pulitzer debacle: "...I'm hardly surprised that my kind of music is still without, let us say, official honor at home. Most Americans still take it for granted that European music—classical music, if you will—is the only real respectable kind. . . .

---

[6] Theodore Strongin, "2 Pulitzer Jurors Resign in Protest," *New York Times* 13 May 1965: 39.
[7] Howard Klein, "Ellington Denied Pulitzer Citation," *New York Times* 5 May 1965: 49.

The word 'jazz' has been part of the problem. It never lost its association with those New Orleans bordellos."[8]

The 35-year-old Marsalis, whose roots are in New Orleans, conjures up a far more distinguished image, and his popular acclaim and his commitment to working with children in educational settings augur well for the future of the music. But the real test will come, not with the predictable lionization of Marsalis, but with the recognition of the countless pioneers and prophets of jazz to whom his music is so thoroughly indebted. The trumpeter himself is doing his part through his work with the Lincoln Center Jazz Orchestra, a repertory ensemble devoted to the performance of classic jazz compositions of the past and present.

"We need the kind of shared commitment that can only come from a citizenry convinced that each person shares in our cultural heritage..."

WILLIAM IVEY, *DIRECTOR*, COUNTRY MUSIC FOUNDATION

Happily, Lincoln Center is not alone in expanding its cultural offerings. The programming of many of the country's major arts institutions has become considerably more varied and reflective of the diversity of American society itself. Although dismissed by some critics as affirmative-action aesthetics, a mere pandering to "political correctness" and ultimately a divisive force in American society, such multicultural (or, more accurately, culturally-specific) programming surely has more to do with our increasingly diverse society—and with our increasingly catholic tastes—than with sectarian politics. No one ever complained about America's politically correct cuisine, and yet the transformation of our culinary landscape, from the days not so long ago when ethnic food meant chop suey, pizza, and an occasional taco, has been nothing short of remarkable. The arts in America are finally catching up with this trend, and if the movement seems "political" and

[8] Nat Hentoff, "This Cat Needs No Pulitzer Prize," *New York Times* 12 Sept. 1965: VI-64.

unsettling to some of its critics, that's only because artists, particularly those who have been waiting in the wings for so long, tend to be more outspoken than restaurateurs.

Bernice Johnson Reagon, founder of the musical ensemble Sweet Honey in the Rock and cultural commentator, in an essay aptly entitled "Battle Stancing," traces support for multicultural programming and culturally specific organizations that began to emerge in the late 60s:

> *Our efforts helped shape these funding initiatives. …Now when the decisionmakers in the arts councils, the foundations, or the endowments get together, they at least ask the question 'What are we going to do about minorities?' They wonder about ethnic representation. But they don't do this because they got up one morning and discovered that we are a part of their society; they ask these questions today because we forced this agenda.*

That "agenda" was easier to accommodate in the decade of the 70s when support for the arts was increasing dramatically in both the public and private sectors. More recently, in the face of cutbacks at the federal level and with generally more competition for arts support overall, the climate is less favorable to some forms of pluralism. "No sooner had our efforts begun to result in funding for more complex cultural constituencies," Reagon adds "than the mainstream institutions themselves began to maneuver to take over the very resources we had, through our lobbying efforts, created. Now when we send proposals, we find ourselves in competition with them."[9]

Thus it may be the increased competition for support, as much as the nature of the art itself, that has fueled many of the controversies over multiculturalism of late. As historian and cultural activist John Kuo Wei Tchen points out, "…we need to understand that pluralism, or this ideology of inclusiveness, has always been premised on the pie getting bigger. In an essentially zero-growth economy that is simultaneously becoming more diverse and more unequal, doesn't the

---

[9] Bernice Johnson Reagon, "'Battle Stancing': To Do Cultural Work in America," in *Voices from the Battlefront: Achieving Cultural Equity*, ed. Marta Moreno Vega and Cheryll Y. Greene, (Trenton, N.J: Africa World Press, 1993) 78.

rhetoric of pluralism get stretched precariously thin?"[10] Judging from the sometimes heated reaction within the arts community itself, the patience of some of the participants is getting stretched thin, too.

The politics of pluralism aside, from the audience's standpoint, there are more forms of expression to choose from than ever before. One indication of the broadening of America's cultural palette is the expanded seasons of such major institutions as Carnegie Hall, Lincoln Center, and the Smithsonian Institution, all of which have established repertory ensembles to perform the neglected masterworks of jazz, and where folk and other traditional forms are also increasingly featured. In a survey of performing arts presenters nationwide, in fact, folk or traditional music ranked third in a list of ten types of music most frequently presented.[11]

At once the well-spring of the field and its basic mode of operation — passing both forms and content from one generation to the next — the folk arts legacy is generally not one that has been addressed by the major institutions that help keep other, more formal traditions in the performing and visual arts alive. "Because the folk arts are normally defined as those traditions which are passed on informally through time within a particular community," observes Elizabeth Peterson in *The Changing Face of Tradition*, "we tend to characterize traditional artists as practicing outside of institutional settings. We think of them as 'non-joiners.'"[12]

At the national level, a handful of major institutions have looked after the folk and traditional arts for several years, including the American Folklife Center at the Library of Congress, and the Center for Folklife Programs and Cultural Studies at the Smithsonian Institution. A private organization, the National Council for the Traditional Arts, has been at this task even longer, producing and presenting touring folk arts programs for over 60 years. Efforts such as the Fund for Folk Culture, supported by the Pew Charitable Trusts, and the Programs for Regional Folklife

[10] John Kuo Wei Tchen, "Rethinking Who We Are: A Basic Discussion of Basic Terms," in *Voices from the Battlefront* 7.

[11] *1995 Profile of Member Organizations* (Washington, DC: Association of Performing Arts Presenters, 1995) 11-22.

[12] Betsy Peterson, *The Changing Face of Tradition: A Report on the Folk and Traditional Arts in the United States* (Washington, DC: National Endowment for the Arts, 1996) 68.

Centers, in which seven regional centers received over $10 million in support from the Lila Wallace-Reader's Digest Fund between 1991 and 1995, have been fostering a more systematic approach to the nation's folk legacy.[13]

Still, by its very nature, the folk arts field remains disparate and decentralized, and the question of preserving its legacy, indeed, of protecting its lifeblood, remains a vital one. A 1991 study of the field revealed that more than 85 percent of the folk artists surveyed teach others their art, often without compensation, and a majority consider "identifying and motivating the next generation of artists" to be a priority.[14] Since 1985, that process has been aided immeasurably by the NEA-sponsored State Apprenticeship Programs, part of a larger folk arts effort at the Endowment that has awarded some 3,700 grants totaling nearly $60 million since its inception in 1978.[15] More than 2,600 apprenticeships have been sponsored by state folk arts programs over the past twelve years. "Traditions covered," writes Susan Auerbach, author of a study of the program, "range from Hispanic santos carving in Colorado to African American quilting in Mississippi and from Franco American fiddling in New Hampshire to Hmong wedding songs in Oregon, with crafts dominating the list." A majority of apprenticeships, she notes, have gone to people of color, with American Indians (20 percent), Asian-Americans/Pacific Islanders (15 percent), Alaska Natives (7 percent) especially well represented. But numbers alone cannot measure the importance of apprenticeships to the folk arts field. Auerbach concludes:

[13] The Fund for Folk Culture offers support and technical assistance for gatherings and conferences that bring together folk artists, tradition bearers, folk cultural specialists, and others engaged in the preservation of grassroots cultural traditions. For more information, contact the fund at P.O. Box 1566, Santa Fe, New Mexico. Regional folklife centers participating in the Lila Wallace-Reader's Digest Fund program include Cityfolk (Dayton, OH), City Lore (New York), Philadelphia Folklore Project, Northwest Folklife (Seattle), Texas Folklife Resources, Vermont Folklife Center, and the Western Folklife Center (Elko, NV).
[14] Peterson, 40.
[15] Part of the Office of Special Projects from 1974 to 1977, the Folk Arts program was incorporated into the Heritage and Preservation Division in 1996. "The Program's most far-reaching impact," writes Elizabeth Peterson, "...may be its initial emphasis on creating a nationwide infrastructure of folk arts programs in partnership with state arts agencies and other organizations across the country. Through this strategy, the Folk Arts Program established an effective means for reaching decentralized and diverse constituencies representing many artistic traditions in rural and urban areas throughout the country." Peterson, 56-57.

The impact of apprenticeship programs reverberates well beyond the artist team and the official grant period. Artists often continue working together. …Communities gain well-trained practitioners, articulate spokespersons, and new organizations like the Maine Indian Basketmakers Alliance. Perhaps most importantly languishing art forms that might otherwise die with their last practitioner gain a new lease on life.[16]

"…THE LEAST DOCUMENTED OF ART FORMS"

In many instances, though, not even broader acceptance or institutional clout ensures one a secure place in the cultural legacy. Martha Graham was one of the most respected American choreographers, and *Appalachian Spring* of 1944 stands as a singular achievement in the performing arts, but dance is a field that by its very nature is ephemeral. Often lacking even the recordings that help keep musical traditions alive, a given work in dance demands special handling if it is to remain extant, a heretofore cumbersome and expensive process that until recently was the exception rather than the rule.

A new venture SAVE AS: DANCE is designed specifically to reverse that trend, and in its formal, collaborative aspects, it may serve as a model for what will become increasingly necessary in other fields: targeted, well funded efforts to lift particular art forms out of the largely untended stockpiles of American culture into the more specialized arenas of preserved, archived, and "contextualized" works. Just as efforts are underway to transfer America's film heritage from disintegrating nitrate stock onto more durable and accessible media, and as "brittle" books are being digitized and made much more widely available in the nation's library system, so will specific efforts on behalf of other art forms be needed—both to rescue given works from unjustified obscurity or neglect, and to document and preserve these works in a context that will allow both artists of today and audiences of tomorrow to understand and appreciate them.

"Dance has been the least documented of art forms," explains Andrea Snyder, director of the National Initiative to Preserve American Dance (NIPAD), based at the John F. Kennedy Center for the Performing Arts in Washington, DC.

---

[16] Susan Auerbach, "Investing in the Future of Tradition: State Apprenticeship Programs," in Peterson, 24, 26. For additional information of the apprenticeship programs, see Auerbach, *In Good Hands: State Apprenticeship Programs in Folk & Traditional Arts, 1983-1995* (Washington, DC: National Endowment for the Arts, 1995).

PHOTO BY TOM CARAVAGLIA

Dancers from Lula Washington Dance Theatre, located in
South Central Los Angeles, in performance. SAVE: AS DANCE is
an initiative to document and preserve this art form.

"By facilitating the documentation and preservation of dance, we hope not only to
spur artistic activity, but also to increase people's appreciation of dance as central to
human activity." Launched in 1993 with the help of support from the Pew
Charitable Trusts, NIPAD has awarded over $1 million in grants for the documen-
tation of a wide range of dance styles, "from Merce Cunningham's 'Torse' to the
court dances of Cambodia, the African-Puerto Rican Bomba, and the dances of the
Tonawanda Band of Seneca Indians in upstate New York," according to a report by
Jennifer Dunning in the *New York Times*.[17] Such choreographic pioneers as Daniel
Nagrin, Bessie Schonberg, Erick Hawkins, and Doris Humphrey are all being
recorded on videotape, thanks to NIPAD-funded projects.

[17] Jennifer Dunning, "An Invitation to Step Into a Formidable Future," *New York Times* 9 Feb. 1997: H-12.

More recently, in conjunction with the UCLA National Dance/Media Project, NIPAD is managing the SAVE AS: DANCE initiative, encompassing a broad range of documentation and preservation activities that includes cataloguing existing materials, preserving deteriorating films and videos, making new audio/visual recordings, and exploring innovative ways to use new media for both creating and disseminating dance works. Awarding larger grants to fewer projects, SAVE AS: DANCE will extend the leadership role of NIPAD and its partner at UCLA by developing model projects, assembling a national advisory body to serve as a "think tank" on documentation, and convening a national conference in 1998 to explore the most advanced techniques and concepts in dance documentation.

Administrators and historians in other fields would do well to consider adopting this kind of systematic approach to the legacy of other art forms. "Dance has at last reached the stage that literature reached with the invention of the printing press," observes Judith Mitoma, founder and director of UCLA's Center for Intercultural Performance in the Department of World Arts and Cultures. "The emergence of so many new technologies enables us to document anything we want. But if we do not use these tools to save our dance history—and to make it more accessible and exciting for the public—Americans will never fully appreciate the contributions of dance to our culture, or be inclined to support it in the future."

"...THESE GUYS ARE DEAD ON ARRIVAL"

And yet there is still more to the cultural legacy than that: even if we manage finally to catch up with the cultural trailblazers like Charles Ives, to honor the unheralded like Clifford Brown, and to rescue the various endangered species of the arts from vanishing altogether, there remains the matter of content—of *conflict*, in fact—involving works that deal unflinchingly with some of the thornier issues of our time. Ours is often a culture of contention, and artists are frequently in the front ranks of those asking difficult questions, exploring difficult terrain.

Such was the case with *Angels in America*, the 1993 theater sensation that continues to reverberate through American culture to this day. With seven Tony awards and a Pulitzer Prize to its credit, it's difficult to recall a more widely acclaimed work than Tony Kushner's two-part opus. Writing in *The New Yorker*, for example, John Lahr called the first part, "Perestroika," a masterpiece, suggesting that "not since [Tennessee] Williams has a playwright announced his poetic vision with such authority on the Broadway stage."[18] Robert Brustein, meanwhile, judged *Angels*' second part, "Millennium Approaches," to be "the authoritative achievement of a radical dramatic artist with a fresh, clear voice," and *Newsweek*'s Jack Kroll called both parts "the broadest, deepest, most searching American play of our time."[19]

But it's never quite as simple as that, and one need look no further than the work's subtitle—A Gay Fantasia on National Themes—to understand why. For included among our "national themes," unfortunately, are intolerance, homophobia, and a fear of diversity and "otherness" which lead to fear and anger. Worse still, sometimes even civic commissions lash out.

That's essentially what happened in Charlotte, NC, in 1997, when the Mecklenberg County Commission, on the strength of a five-to-four vote, raised tyranny of the majority to new heights by withholding $2.5 million in county funds earmarked for the Arts and Science Council of Charlotte/Mecklenberg County, vowing to allocate that money directly to arts groups according to its own, more restrictive, criteria. The Arts and Science Council, whose overall budget is around $11 million, had supported the Charlotte Repertory Theatre in years past, and it was this company that had presented, amidst much controversy in the spring of 1996, *Angels in America*.

Initially targeting the Arts and Science Council for "recognizing and supporting homosexuality," the county commissioners finally settled on a resolution that barred public funds from supporting groups that present "perverted forms of sexuality," or that "promote, advocate or endorse behaviors, life styles and values that seek to undermine and deviate from the value and societal role of the traditional family."[20] However general the language, the commission's specific intentions were laid bare during the course of its deliberations. "As far as I'm concerned, these guys are dead on arrival," explained one commissioner, in reference to the Charlotte Repertory Theatre. "If they don't know they're the walking dead now, I suggest they get a clue pretty quick."[21]

---

[18] John Lahr, "The Theatre: Earth Angels," *The New Yorker* 13 Dec. 1993: 133.
[19] Robert Brustein, "Robert Brustein on Theatre: Angels in America," *The New Republic* 24 May 1993: 29; Jack Kroll, "Heaven and Earth on Broadway," *Newsweek* 6 Dec. 1993: 83.
[20] "County Strikes at Arts Council Over Gay Play," *New York Times* 3 Apr. 1997: A17.
[21] *Charlotte Observer* 3 Apr. 1997.

Ironically, what began as an effort to target a specific group may spill over into other areas, including arts education. Nearly half of the funds that were headed to the Arts and Science Council, some $1.2 million, was destined for Spirit Square, the city-owned theater that is being converted into an arts education center. Also jeopardized by the county commission's action is the arts council's partnership with the school district, which was planning to use *The Wizard of Oz* to teach reading, math, writing, and art skills. Some commission members who voted against the resolution expressed their opposition to seeing the commission itself becoming the arbiter of taste in matters of arts funding (a view shared by some 85 percent of county residents in a *Charlotte Observer* poll), and may decide to eliminate arts funding altogether.

The battle in Charlotte is typical of debates underway elsewhere, concerning the responsibility of the public patron, especially in resolving the conflict between national standards and local politics, between First Amendment freedoms and public accountability. The Charlotte episode is also a not-so-subtle reminder that there is no "sure thing" when it comes to matters of art. Kushner won't be silenced by a county commission, of course, but other artists might not be so fortunate. Writers such as Bernard Gordon and the late Hugo Butler doubtless had higher aspirations for their work in the 1950s, and certainly could not have predicted what 1997 would bring: an effort, tragically belated, to restore their names to film projects on which they were forced to use pseudonyms during the era of blacklisting in Hollywood.[22]

"...OUR COLLECTIVE MEMORY..."

These four examples outline the complex nature of our "cultural legacy," discussions of which ran through many of the American Canvas forums, if not directly in frank discussions of the danger of losing vital parts of our cultural past, then obliquely in subtle undercurrents of doubt concerning the financial health of the nonprofit sector and the concomitant risk of losing sight of both the past and the future in the daily struggle to survive in the present.

Participants in the American Canvas forum in Charlotte tackled the question of the legacy head on, stressing the need, in particular, to define that legacy in

[22] Bernard Weinraub, "Blacklisted Writers Win Credits for Screenplays," *New York Times* 3 Apr. 1997: B1.

terms sufficiently broad to embrace the full extent of American culture. For William Ivey, executive director of the Country Music Foundation, legacy is "that part of the past we intend to keep for the future." Ellen Lovell, former executive director of the President's Committee on the Arts and Humanities, agreed, citing "our collective memory," which runs the full gamut from personal identity and language to songs, crafts, even historic districts that we collectively agree to protect from the ravages of time (or the rapacity of developers, which can be equally destructive). The key, Lovell observed, is *authenticity*. Many American Canvas forum participants, including George Rivera of the Poeh Cultural Center and Museum north of Santa Fe (celebrating the Tewa-speaking Pueblos) and Dorothy Jenkins Fields of Historic Overtown (the turn-of-the-century segregated community that later became a thriving center of African-American culture in Miami), offered examples of efforts to preserve authentic examples of our collective history. Commercial re-creations of the past, it was generally agreed, be they Hollywood evocations of days gone by or quaint theme-park villages, ultimately prove to be hollow experiences, in comparison to the real thing.

The commercial sector, even in the eyes of those who operate in that arena, comes up short as the protector of our cultural legacy. According to Michael Greene, president of the National Academy of Recording Arts and Sciences and a participant at the Los Angeles forum, a decidedly public perspective, maintained at the federal level, is needed to direct the effort of preserving the past. "We have to have a federal presence to really think in the longer view about where our society as a whole is going," Greene declared. "…[A] national consciousness has to always be there in some form or fashion to understand that the mercantile, commercial aspects of art have nothing to do with the legacy, necessarily."

It's not that nothing worth saving emanates from the commercial sector. On the contrary, one of the greatest strengths of American culture, and a primary reason for its vast appeal abroad, is the imagination and boundless energy of our popular artists. One need only point to the body of recorded music in this century, or the classic films of Hollywood, to recognize the importance of this sector. Yet the entertainment industry, more concerned with dividends than with any legacy it might leave, does not have a distinguished record in preserving its past, beyond those items, anyway, that continue to have a value in the marketplace.

"...THE PEOPLE HERE ARE REAL"

Whether or not one shares Greene's faith in federal action in this area, the belief
that cultural preservation should represent a collective effort, rather than strictly a
business proposition, seems undeniable. As William Ivey, who has dedicated his
career to the study and appreciation of country and western music, expressed it in
Charlotte, "We really need the kind of shared commitment that can only come
from a citizenry convinced that each person shares in our cultural heritage, and that
they have a stake in it, and it's important to our society, and that it is as vital as the
air we breathe." It is the responsibility of the present generation, added Joe
Wilson, executive director of the National Council on the Traditional Arts, "to preserve and transmit our historic culture, and to do so in a way that both encompasses the breadth of that culture and builds the kinds of alliances that are needed to
keep that legacy alive."

Unilateral efforts to preserve the past, whether for commercial gain or for
purely altruistic motives, are not likely to succeed. Wilson offered the example of
Lowell, Massachusetts, a one-time mill town that has managed both to recapture its
past and to revitalize its present in the form of an annual arts festival that attracts
more than 200,000 visitors annually to a town of less than half that size. But none
of this happened overnight.

Lowell's own legacy is one of both triumph and travail, as the city har-
nessed the power of the Merrimack River and its many canals to win some of the
initial battles of the Industrial Revolution in the 19th century, only to witness the
eventual closing of its cotton mills early in the next century, as the center of textile
manufacturing shifted to the Southern states. "Lowell had a bad reputation
throughout the region," Wilson recalls. "It was the kind of place, if you wanted to
insult your girlfriend, you told her you were taking her there on a date."

The city's renewed self-confidence came slowly, and the arts and culture
played a central role in the rebuilding process. First came the small ethnic festivals,
literally hundreds of them over the years, drawing on the rich cultural diversity that
has long distinguished Lowell, home to no less than 52 distinct ethnic groups.
While many of these groups, including the Irish, French Canadian, Portuguese, and
Greeks, trace their roots in Lowell back to the flush times of the nineteenth century, more recent arrivals, including over 25,000 from Cambodia, Laos, and Vietnam,
found their way to Lowell because of upheaval in their homelands.

The city's self-image got another boost when it finally came to terms with
its own past, when it began to celebrate rather than shun, in other words, both the

peaks and the valleys of its own heritage. At the heart of this new outlook was the Lowell National Historical Park, created in 1978 to proclaim the city's role in the Industrial Revolution, and which transformed neglected mill complexes, gatehouses, power canals, and other erstwhile relics from Lowell's past into a living museum of industrial history.

In 1987, finally, Wilson's National Council on the Traditional Arts (NCTA) selected Lowell as the site for its National Folk Festival, a 63-year-old movable feast of the traditional arts and crafts that spent three years there (1987-89) before moving on to Johnstown, Pennsylvania. Building on the momentum of that event, and drawing on the city's own storied past, the city launched its own festival, which celebrated its 10th anniversary last year as the largest free festival of its kind in the country. A partnership of the city, the National Historical Park, the Festival Foundation, and Wilson's NCTA, the Lowell Folk Festival has grown in popularity every year. The city itself spends some $60,000 on the event every year, although that figure would swell to over $100,000 if all of the volunteer labor were factored into the equation. "It's money that is well spent," according to Ed Trudel, operations director of the city of Lowell. "The public relations the city gets from this event cannot be measured it's so great."

Judging from the popular reaction—visitors from all over New England and the East Coast descend on Lowell the last weekend in July—Trudel's accounting is accurate. "I thought it was an old-time mill town that was all run down," a visitor from Charlestown, MA, told the Lowell *Sun* last year, "and I've heard about drug problems and things like that, but it's like a garden. It's just gorgeous." The man's wife was equally impressed: "... the people here are real. It's such a nice mix of people, it restores your faith in America. I know that sounds sappy and very 'American Pie,' but it's really true."[23]

"...WE REALLY NEED TO START WORKING TODAY FOR TOMORROW"

Sappy or no, that couple from Charlestown captured the essence of what these kinds of cultural programs, from the smallest downtown arts festival to such massive undertakings as the Lowell event, attempt to do: "to provide us the means," as

[23] Laura Doyle, "Record crowd savors Folk Fest sights, smells, sounds," *The Sun* (Lowell, MA) 29 July 1996: 8.

Anna White of Young Audiences of Indiana said at the Columbus American Canvas forum, "to express and preserve our cultural heritage, and to respond and work with those who have lost the sense of pride and hope in our communities today." The Lowell Folk Festival embodies that very process, retrieving elements of our varied cultural past, bringing them alive in the present, and helping to ensure, along the way, that Irish step dancing, Andean music, Laotian handicrafts and other traditions will live into the future.

Like the curiously intricate concept of legacy itself, such efforts as SAVE AS: DANCE and the Lowell Folk Festival have as much to do with the future as they do with the past, although in our preoccupation with not letting the latter slip through our fingers, we sometimes lose sight of the future, failing to account for the current generation of artists who, given half a chance, might one day contribute to our cultural legacy. The Dayton-Hudson Foundation's Ben Cameron raised that very issue at the Columbus forum—"The complete question is how do you preserve the achievements of the past while still recognizing the aspirations and ambitions of a rising and incipient generation."

"We have to support the developing artists of today, in order to have a legacy tomorrow," National Endowment for the Arts Chairman Jane Alexander pointed out in Charlotte, "because you think about composers who, on average, do not reach their peak of fame or production of their works until 50 years after their death. So, we really need to start working today for tomorrow."

THE EVOLVING CULTURAL LANDSCAPE

The nonprofit arts, Jane Alexander observed at the American Canvas forum in Salt Lake City, have been hit with a "triple whammy" in recent years, with cutbacks in funding at the federal, state, and local levels. The private sector, meanwhile, faced with increasing demands on its resources, has not been able to compensate for these reductions. Other American Canvas participants pointed to other factors, including the many social problems that the arts have been asked to address, that contribute to the changing cultural landscape of the United States.

Unfortunately, our grasp of these changing conditions is limited by the existing state of cultural statistics, which offer only rudimentary approximations of the data we would ideally have at our disposal. "In attempting to use existing data systems to track critical ongoing transformations in the arts," observe Deborah Kaple and Paul DiMaggio, two scholars who are working to improve our view of the arts infrastructure, "we are like the drunk who looks for his lost wallet under the lamp-post because 'that's where the light is best.'"[1]

[1] Paul DiMaggio and Deborah Kaple, "Information on Arts Organizations," *Grantmakers in the Arts* 7 (Autumn 1996) 13.

If nothing else, though, the existing data on the nonprofit arts suggest the predicament: increases in the number of artists and arts organizations over the past three decades has far outpaced the growth in both public and private support, which rose dramatically in the 60s and 70s before leveling off (and actually declining in the case of federal support) in the 80s and 90s. But even these statistics tend to hide as much as they reveal.

The figures for arts organizations, for example, which show remarkable growth rates in the fields of orchestras, theaters, opera, and dance companies, are limited to the professional, tax-exempt, 501(C)(3) universe of organizations that qualify for support from public and private funders.[2] Fields in which nonprofit incorporation is less common (jazz and chamber music, for example) fall outside of these figures, as do the myriad occasional, amateur, and student aggregations that nevertheless help bring the arts to millions of Americans every year.

Similarly, the definition of "artists in the workforce" (the size of which more than doubled, from 720,000 to 1,671,000, between 1970 and 1990), is that of the Census Bureau.[3] That definition includes radio and television announcers and teachers of art, drama, and music in higher education, but it doesn't account for part-time artists, the bulk of whose income may come from private teaching or other pursuits, but whose contributions to American culture, over the entire span of their careers, can be considerable. Nor is amateur arts activity accounted for, although that may have a greater—if less measurable—impact on our culture than previously imagined. Audience figures for the arts, similarly, are skewed toward the formal definitions of the seven types of arts activities included in the Survey of Public Participation of the Arts—a useful index of Americans' behavior in certain formal areas of the nonprofit arts, but far from a complete inventory of arts participation (which, again, includes extensive hands-on activity in music, photography, and dance, for example, which we've been too quick to dismiss as merely avocational pursuits in the past).

[2] According to figures released by the National Endowment for the Arts' Office of Communications, the number of professional opera companies has grown from 27 to 120 between 1965 and 1994, the number of professional orchestras from 100 to 230, dance companies from 37 to 400, and theater companies from 56 to 425.

[3] Neil O. Alper and Gregory H. Wassall, et al, *Artists in the Workforce: Employment and Earnings, 1970-1990* (Santa Ana, CA: Seven Locks Press) 3.

More accurate, if still fragmentary, are the figures for private support of the arts—in the range of $10 billion every year—in which tax-deductible cash and in-kind contributions are easier to track than other forms of support, particularly from the corporate sector (e.g., non-deductible advertising expenses that benefit the arts, or personnel loaned to arts organizations). More significantly, these figures tell us nothing about the distribution patterns of private sector support. While public expenditures in the arts can be traced down to the smallest organizational or individual recipients, the reporting requirements for private philanthropy are not nearly so rigorous.

Nevertheless, scattered reports from the front lines of the nonprofit culture tend to confirm the lamp-post trend lines discussed here. A 1995 survey of 174 member institutions of the Association of Art Museum Directors, for example, revealed expenses that amounted to $30 per museum visitor on average (with an average $1.45 admission fee). Public-sector contributions totaling $281 million, along with $372 million in private-sector contributions, helped make up the deficit, but overall these museums reported an income shortfall of 22 percent.[4] Similarly, Dance/USA's survey of the 65 largest dance companies in the country (out of more than 600 nationally), all with budgets over $1 million, reported total expenses of $257 million and total incomes of $163.7 million, a 36 percent deficit.[5] Opera America's universe is both smaller (112 companies in 41 states) and more diverse (from Amarillo Opera's $174,000 budget to the Metropolitan Opera's $134 million), but nearly half of these companies reported a deficit during the 1994-95 season.[6] Theatre Communications Group's 1995 survey of 215 theaters, finally, offered the brightest picture, but here, too, the financial picture was mixed: just over half of the theaters reported operating fund surpluses, but collectively, the theaters ran a slight deficit ($552,344, or 0.12 percent).[7]

"...AN ANOMALY IN AMERICAN PUBLIC LIFE"

These reports from the field illuminate what's going on in the major leagues of the nonprofit culture, certainly, but the arts universe is far larger than the high-profile

[4] Association of Art Museum Directors, "Field at a Glance: Art Museums," press release, n.d. [1996].
[5] Dance/USA, "Field at a Glance: Dance," press release, n.d. [1996].
[6] Opera America, "Field at a Glance: Opera," press release, n.d. [1996].
[7] Theatre Communications Group, "Theatre Facts 1995," American Theater Apr. 1996: 2-3.

institutions alone. And far harder to track. Equally frustrating, especially for anyone attempting to assess some of the qualitative aspects of American culture—who's doing what kind of work, to what end, and how their efforts measure up against earlier generations of artists—is the lack of a reliable analytical system and a forum in which to launch such an undertaking.

A recent study of the current state of cultural data, sponsored by the Arts Endowment and undertaken by Kaple, DiMaggio, and others at Princeton University's Center for Arts and Cultural Policy Statistics (CACPS), recommends the development of a "Unified Data Base" for the nonprofit arts in America to find data that are comparable across different organizational types, distinct disciplines, and over time. Invariably, among the chronically under-represented in such reporting are small, community-based, cross-disciplinary, experimental, ad hoc, and/or "underground" organizations, precisely where much of the most compelling work in the arts today is being undertaken. Nor will "virtual" groups that are now being fashioned online be recognized in standard data-collection sweeps, although such groups may play an increasingly important role on the emerging cultural landscape.

Equally important, those crucial questions about the direction of American culture—the nature of programming, the quality of performances and exhibitions, the vital linkages between and among arts and nonarts organizations, and the many contributions the arts make far beyond the aesthetic—will initially go unanswered. Nevertheless, the kind of coordinated, systematic, open-ended data collection that the CACPS study calls for, drawing on a variety of existing and projected data sources, offers the best chance we have of arriving at something we currently lack: a reliable, comprehensive overview of the nonprofit arts universe. For that unified data base to become a reality, however, there will have to be an even greater change in the way the arts community currently conducts its affairs, with a level of foresight, cooperation, and information sharing that has not always existed in this sector.

"...VITAL TO OUR...SELF-IMAGE"

In the meantime, economists James Heilbrun and Charles M. Gray, in their useful study of the field, *The Economics of Art and Culture: An American Perspective*, offer one of the best vantage points from which to view the nonprofit arts universe. Heilbrun and Gray are very much aware that there is more to the arts economy than the mere exchange of money for aesthetic goods and services. If that's all it

The Philadelphia Orchestra performs before an enthusiastic audience
in Ann Arbor at the University of Michigan.

were, they point out, the stakes would be minuscule indeed. The estimated $4.31
billion that Americans spent on admissions to live, nonprofit performing arts events
in 1990, for example, may sound like a lot, but it's less than half of what Americans
paid for flowers, seeds, and potted plants that year. Even when the operating
incomes of art museums are added to the mix, along with all public and private
contributions to the arts, the nonprofit arts economy in 1990—conservatively estimated by Heilbrun and Gray to be $7.3 billion—is only slightly more than one-
thousandth of the gross domestic product (0.133 percent).[8] The nonprofit arts
industry, the two economists concede, "is very small in relation to the U.S. economy. Why, then, do we study it? Obviously we do so because it is vital to our culture, and therefore to our self-image."[9]

[8] James Heilbrun and Charles M. Gray, *The Economics of Art and Culture: An American Perspective* (New York: Cambridge University Press, 1993) 7-9.
[9] Heilbrun and Gray, *Economics* 10.

In addition to putting the nonprofit arts economy into perspective, Heilbrun and Gray also shed light on its relative health as measured by consumer demand for the arts. Lending credence to the often touted "cultural boom" of the years following the creation of the Arts Endowment, Heilbrun and Gray note the growth in consumer spending on the live performing arts: between 1975 and 1990, expenditures grew from 6.8 cents per $100 of disposable personal income (DPI) to 12.3 cents. Viewed from another vantage point, though, such spending was actually higher in 1929 (15.5 cents), before declining irregularly thereafter (attributable initially to the advent of talking pictures and later to television). *The Economics of Art and Culture* is not optimistic about the prospects of the post-1975 "cultural boom" continuing, pointing both to the supply-side factors that are impossible to maintain indefinitely (i.e., the rapid growth in the number of arts organizations, fueled by increased public and private contributions during these years), and an actual downturn in consumer demand in 1991, when "the dollar amount of consumer spending for admissions to the live performing arts fell five percent..., registering its first significant year-to-year decline since 1948."[10] Annual growth of the nonprofit arts sector may have come to an end.

> *Attendance at symphony concerts rose to a peak of 25.4 million in 1986, declined to 22.4 million by 1989, and then leveled off at 22.3 million in 1991. Several orchestras in medium-sized cities collapsed financially in the late 1980s but were brought back to life under new auspices; one—the Oakland Symphony—went down for good. Workweeks under the Actors' Equity contract with the League of Resident Theatres (LORT) reached a level of 62,397 in 1989 and then fell to 58,369 in 1991. The number of ballet companies declined from 331 in 1986 to 281 in 1992. Although attendance at main seasons and festival performances of major opera companies continued to rise through the 1989-90 season..., the amount of touring activity began to fall off.[11]*

More recently, of course, the precipitous decline in federal arts support, accompanied by volatility at the state level, have added to the general state of con-

---

[10] Heilbrun and Gray, *Economics* 21.
[11] Heilbrun and Gray, *Economics* 20-21.

sternation in the arts community. As former Ohio Governor Richard Celeste observed at the Columbus American Canvas forum, the arts "can no longer expect first-dollar support from the public sector," a reference to the declining role that government agencies—never a majority partner in the arts-support enterprise in any case—would be playing in this regard. "There must be strong community support first," Celeste advised. "A basic part of the arts is independence, a willingness to engender controversy, to challenge the way we think—all factors that may affect the effort to develop community support."

FOUNDATION SUPPORT

Conventional wisdom in the arts suggests that the most recent lean times are anomalous, merely a temporary setback. However one demarcates those "lean times"—the leveling off of federal arts funding that began in the early 1980s, or the political squabbles that broke out later in that decade, or the draconian cuts in the Arts Endowment budget that Congress exacted in 1996 and sustained in 1997— better times are surely ahead, or so the argument runs, a moderated Renaissance Lite will one day return.

More recently, however, a growing number of observers have begun to suggest that it was this earlier, "golden" age that may have been anomalous. A combination of related factors—uncharacteristically generous public and private funders, a growing population of under-compensated artists and administrators, and an artificially high birth-rate for nonprofit arts organizations—aligned themselves to produce a uniquely fertile period for the nation's nonprofit culture.

For arts writer John Kreidler, a veteran of both public and private arts funding agencies of over 25 years, a critical moment of post-war American culture was the emergence of the Ford Foundation as a major arts patron, making more than $400 million in arts grants between 1957 and 1976, and helping to launch the nonprofit arts sector that mushroomed during the 1960s and 1970s. "Until the arrival of the Ford Foundation's broad vision of arts funding," Kreidler observes, "virtually all cultural philanthropy had been vested with individuals and generally lacked any strategic intent."[12] The Ford Foundation's "strategic intent" encompassed

[12] John Kreidler, "Leverage Lost: The Nonprofit Arts in the Post-Ford Era," *The Journal of Arts Management, Law and Society* 26 (Summer 1996): 82.

both the revitalization and stabilization of major nonprofit arts institutions, targeting orchestras, theaters, and dance companies in particular, and setting in motion a cultural decentralization campaign that would later figure prominently in the federal government's arts program that began in 1965. "It is highly significant," Kreidler adds,

that the Ford Foundation viewed itself as a catalyst for these major developments but not as a perpetual funder. The majority of Ford's grants were limited to less than five years' duration and required matching support two to four times greater than the amount awarded by the Foundation. So, even though Ford was attempting to increase the capacity of arts organizations to manage themselves on a fiscally sound basis and increase program output, the assumption was that other sources of money, both contributed and earned, would support long-term maintenance.[13]

The impressive growth curves, common across all arts disciplines and reaching into neighborhoods and communities that had little experience with such institutional growth, represented an era of expansion that simply could not be maintained. "The most obvious, though rarely acknowledged, reason that it could not last indefinitely," Kreidler explains, "was that the institutional money supply could not continue to grow."[14]

That money supply alone was not sufficient, in any case, to fuel the non-profit arts sector's precipitous growth. Kreidler cites a number of other social and economic factors of the period, none more important than the highly discounted wage structure that has long characterized the arts in America. "Although the Ford Foundation and NEA deserve much credit for their early support of the nonprofit arts movement," Kreidler observes, "by far the most significant factor in the movement's origin and rapid build-up was the arrival in the 1960s of a huge generation of artists, technicians, and administrators, driven not by funding or economic gain, but rather by their own desire to produce art."[15] In 1960, the Labor Department's *Occupational Outlook Handbook* cautioned against a career in the arts, "The difficulty of earning a living as a performer, is one of the facts young people should

[13] Kreidler, "Leverage Lost" 83.
[14] Kreidler, "Leverage Lost" 91.
[15] Kreidler, "Leverage Lost" 87.

bear in mind in considering an artistic career...It is important for them to consider the possible advantages of making their art a hobby rather than a field of work."[16]

Available employment and earnings data from the period, in any event, support Kreidler's thesis: between 1970 and 1980, the number of art workers increased by 48 percent, while their earnings during this period decreased by 37 percent.[17] "Abundant cheap labor and institutional funding," Kreidler concludes, "were the defining elements of the Ford era; reversals in these two resources are now defining the post-Ford era. Despite remarkable successes in preserving and advancing American high art under the nonprofit banner, the Ford era could not be sustained."[18]

If the nonprofit arts community is painted into a corner, any number of escape routes from these close quarters have been proposed. Many of these routes will be charted later in this report:

~ Increased involvement of the arts in community and civic affairs, generating revenues from areas that are not typically engaged in supporting the arts (e.g., youth programs, crime prevention, economic development).

~ Inclusion of arts education in the basic K-12 curriculum, providing both immediate payoffs, in the form of work for artists and arts organizations in educational activities, and long-term dividends, in the larger audiences that will begin graduating from high schools and colleges in the next century.

~ Expanded marketing efforts, building audiences by appealing more directly to the general public, generating increased earned income in the process.

~ Partnerships with the commercial sector, where the conglomerates of the entertainment industry often spend more money in a day than many nonprofits do in a year.

~ Forays into the electronic frontier, where new digital delivery systems promise to bring a wealth of material (including the arts, presumably) into American homes.

[16] Quoted in U.S. Congress, House, Economic Conditions of the Performing Arts. Hearings before the Select Subcommittee on Education of the Committee on Education and Labor, 87th Cong. 1st and 2nd Sess. (1961-62) 435.

[17] Richard Harvey Brown, "Art as a Commodity," in *The Modern Muse: The Support and Condition of Artists*, ed. C. Richard Swaim (New York: ACA Books, 1989) 19, 20.

[18] Kreidler, "Leverage Lost" 90.

"The example of Spoleto Festival's success has been

an inspiration in our state and throughout America.

We have shown that an arts festival can be a catalyst

for a magnificent renaissance that transforms a city,

its people and economy..."

JOSEPH RILEY, MAYOR, CITY OF CHARLESTON, SOUTH CAROLINA

Despite all of these prospects, the $10 billion annually of private contributions to the arts will remain at the core of the nonprofit arts economy. Especially in comparison to public patrons, private foundations, individual donors and corporate funders continue to hold the key to the health of the nonprofit sector.

Unfortunately, the private sector has not exactly leapt to the rescue of the arts in the face of public-sector cutbacks in the 1990s. Even before the significant budget cuts over the past two years, public arts funding at both the federal and state levels had experienced downturns, with the Arts Endowment budget losing nine percent in real value between 1989 and 1992, and the states collectively losing twice that amount in the same period. Foundation giving to the arts during these years (the latest of four triennial periods studied by the Foundation Center) may have grown 12 percent in constant dollars, but it failed to keep pace with the growth of private philanthropy overall (which rose 14 percent in real value). The share of arts funding, moreover, dropped slightly during that three-year period, from 13.6 percent to 13.3 percent.[19]

More recently (and again, adjusting for inflation), all private support for the arts (including foundations, corporations, and individuals) has declined slightly from an all-time high of $10.23 billion in 1992 to just under $10 billion in 1995, the first triennium of no or negative growth in the 31 years that such statistics

---

[19] Loren Renz, *Arts Funding Revisited: An Update on Foundation Trends in the 1990s* (New York: The Foundation Center, 1995) 2-3.

have been kept.[20] But the news might not be all bad. Aside from the somewhat unsettling fact that the arts managed only to hold steady in 1995 while the rest of the philanthropic sector grew by nearly eight percent, it might be said that giving to the arts has gradually "matured" into a less volatile field. Between 1965 and 1995, private giving as a whole rose by more than six percent only twice (in 1986 and 1995) and fell by more than three percent only once (1970). The arts, in contrast, had 12 such leaps in the first 22 years of that period, but only one in the past nine.[21]

Arts philanthropy, ultimately, is affected by a number of factors, including competition with other parts of the nonprofit sector (of which public/society benefit and education have shown the most growth in recent years), and, more generally, the impact of the economy on charitable giving as a whole. Given the many social challenges facing American society, it's unlikely that the competition for funding will be any less keen any time soon.

The road of arts philanthropy is likely to be a bumpy one over the next several years, but with fewer sharp peaks and valleys than in the past. The real question, though, is whether the leading arts funders (including the 25 largest foundations that provide 40 percent of all arts funding from that sector) can be persuaded to navigate this terrain in a more open and coordinated manner, less dependent on the strong will of patrons acting independently, more accommodating of the collective wisdom of an arts community that will simply have to pull together if it hopes to flourish in the next century.

Community foundations may lead the way in this regard, adding a much needed element of public policy to a field that has long been dominated by laissez-faire practices. There are now more than 400 community foundations across the country, devoting nearly 17 percent of their funding to the arts (for a total of more than $40 million in 1995). A number of them are working with a national funder, the Lila Wallace-Reader's Digest Fund, whose new $15 million initiative, "Community Partnerships for Cultural Participation," targets the need to increase public participation in the arts. Both in its collaborative aspects, and in its com-

---

[20] AAFRC Trust for Philanthropy, *Giving USA: The Annual Report on Philanthropy for the Year 1995* (New York: AAFRC, 1996) 25. Only once before, in 1977-78, has private support for the arts declined in two consecutive years.

[21] AAFRC, *Giving USA* 24-15.

mitment to sharing information with the field, this new program may turn out to be a model private philanthropic effort.

CORPORATE PHILANTHROPY

"The merchant should be a patron of the arts," Judge James Hall told a group of young Cincinnati businessmen in 1846.[22] While it took the business community as a whole over a century to heed that advice, the corporate sector eventually became a major supporter of the arts, making upwards of $750 million available to arts organizations every year. And there may be more where that came from. Only half of all businesses that give to nonprofits support the arts. Among the more disturbing trends in this sector, on the other hand, is the 21 percent decline in the share of corporate philanthropy devoted to the arts in recent years, from 11.8 percent in 1992 to 9.3 percent in 1995.[23]

Corporate support of the arts has historically mirrored the rise in public expenditures. In 1965, for example, the share of the corporate philanthropic dollar devoted to the arts was only 2.8 percent. A decade later, in 1975, it had reached 7.5 percent, breaking the 10 percent barrier five years later. As late as 1969, corporate patron Kenneth Dayton still viewed business support of the arts as a hedge against an expanding public sector. "In the absence of such support," Dayton declared, "government will do the whole job (or at least try to do it) and then will raise corporate and individual taxes to pay the additional costs."[24] True to his word, by 1969 Dayton's department store empire was midway through what would become a 50-year record of donating a full five percent of pre-tax profits to charitable causes.[25]

Nearly three decades later, with government arts support declining and with talk of tax cuts rather than increases now the norm, the Dayton Hudson

---

[22] Quoted in Freeman Hunt, *Worth and Wealth: A Collection of Maxims, Morals, and Miscellanies for Merchants and Men of Business* (New York: Stringer & Townsend, 1856) 220.

[23] Conference Board, *Corporate Contributions in 1995: A Research Report* (New York: Conference Board, 1996).

[24] Quoted in Arnold Gingrich, *Business and the Arts: An Answer to Tomorrow* (New York, P.S. Eriksson, 1969) 42.

[25] "Dayton Hudson Corporation's 5% Philanthropic Tradition Turns 50," *The Chronicle of Philanthropy* (11 July 1996). Between 1936 and 1981, companies were permitted to deduct up to five percent of taxable income as contributions. Although this ceiling was raised to ten percent in 1981, historically the average for all companies has been closer to one percent.

Foundation's senior program officer for the arts, Ben Cameron, offered a more confident appraisal of the arts-and-business nexus. As part of his participation at the American Canvas forum in Columbus, Cameron crafted a five-part rationale for Dayton Hudson's strong commitment to the arts, touching on historical precedent, quality-of-life and economic implications, the societal benefits of creativity, and, inevitably, the "enlightened self-interest" that has long been the driving force behind most corporate philanthropy. Far from offering a magic formula, though, Cameron's observations are much closer to an agenda for an arts community that may need to turn increasingly to the business sector for support in the future.

"Historically," Cameron began, "the founding family [of Dayton Hudson] was (and is) keenly committed to the arts. Their guidance led us to a strong role in the arts community, a legacy we find valuable and are reluctant to dismiss." While that commitment remains strong at a large, privately held company like Dayton Hudson, the same cannot necessarily be claimed for other parts of the corporate sector, in which mergers, downsizing, and the entry of a new managerial corps, (the first of a generation whose formal training was more likely to have been focused on specialized business skills than on a broad liberal arts tradition) all play a role. The same concerns that have been raised about audiences for the arts, in other words, whose younger members are less likely to be committed to the arts than their parents, can be applied to the corporate sector.

Second, according to Cameron, getting closer to the heart of cultural programs' attraction for business, "the arts create more livable communities." The potential economic implications of this aspect of corporate giving should not go unnoticed. The recent downturn in the share of business support going to the arts, for example, can be traced at least in part to the increased interest in community affairs, which grew 11 percent between 1993 and 1995 alone.[26]

The third of Cameron's five-point rationale is that "the arts are key components in the economic vitality of any community," a theme that generates more excitement among business and civic leaders alike than any other. Here, finally, are the kind of measurable results—1.3 million workers in the nonprofit arts, generat-

---

[26] Long tied to the standard philanthropic targets in health, education, and welfare, business giving gradually started to become more variegated in the decade of the sixties. The "civic and culture" category (a mere 5.3 percent percent in 1962) branched into separate entries for each in 1965, and eventually grew to between 9-12 percent each.

ing $37 billion in economic activity, and returning $3.4 billion to the treasury in income taxes—that even non-afficianados can appreciate.[27] Translated to the local level—and business philanthropy, it should be noted, is overwhelmingly local, tied as it is to markets and plant locations—economic impact studies have become a major weapon in the arts fundraiser's arsenal. But however persuasive these bottom-line arguments may be, it must also be acknowledged that they are based on a premise that is ultimately a losing proposition. Simply put, the Juilliard String Quartet will never have the *economic* impact of the Smashing Pumpkins, no more than the Boston Symphony Orchestra will ever serve as many people as the Boston Market restaurant chain.

In his fourth point, Cameron stated "that the arts advance creativity, which has resonance far beyond the arts themselves. Especially as our society begins to address formidable social problems, the value of creative thinking is key to our collective success." A number of other American Canvas participants shared this view, urging artists and arts organizations "to bring their processes as well as their products to the table," in their efforts to integrate arts activities into civic and community affairs.

"Giving back is, quite simply, the right thing to do," Cameron concluded. "Obviously, corporate giving has a dimension of self-interest: more livable communities attract better workers, and greater economic vitality means customers capable of higher spending." But there is an increasing danger of the arts gradually sliding further and further down the list of priorities for the ever-more-competitive philanthropic dollar, as corporate mergers and takeovers alter the character of a company's leadership, and as a generation emerges lacking both the educational background and thinking and perceptual skills that make them less capable of receiving and appreciating our nation's cultural legacy. "And more and more of this critical issue," Cameron added, "is borne out by our surveys where the allegiance to the arts tends to decline the younger the generation."

Dayton Hudson's approach to corporate philanthropy, both in its generosity and in its sophisticated grasp of the needs of the arts nationally, stands as a model for others in the field. The overall trend, however, appears to favor a more rationalized approach, as multinational operations, facing an ever-more-competitive global marketplace, feel compelled to stress profits over personality. "The last sever-

---

[27] National Assembly of Local Arts Agencies. *Economic Impact of the Arts* (1994).

al years," Nina Kressner Cobb points out in *Looking Ahead,* a report on private philanthropy commissioned by the President's Committee on the Arts and the Humanities, "have witnessed a major shift in corporate giving to the arts. In the late 80s, responsibility for setting policy for giving to the arts began to move from corporate-giving departments to marketing, advertising, public relations, and human resources department and become much more market-driven."[28]

It's too early to tell how that kind of shift will affect corporate philanthropy, perhaps, although Robert Fitzpatrick, for one, expects the worst. "Corporate giving, which began as a CEO's gesture of good citizenship and whose only payback was community good will," the former president of California Institute for the Arts and director of the Los Angeles Olympics Arts Festival suggests, "is now increasingly determined by directors of marketing and sales. Cause-related marketing is the most recent perversion of philanthropy: I expect the next American Express ad to say: 'Charge your Christmas shopping at Tiffany's and we will contribute a dime to a starving artist.' America has moved from frequent flyer miles to feel-good points."[29]

That jaundiced view of corporate philanthropy has long been common in the nonprofit sector, and as such it sheds little light on the arts-and-business nexus But the giving-as-advertising trend does bear watching. "Corporate support is not uninterested dollars," observes Ruby Lerner, executive director of the Association of Independent Video and Filmmakers. "It's extremely, specifically, interested dollars..." The danger, she adds, is that ours will soon become a "corporatized culture," in which only those organizations that conform to corporate marketing profiles— "generally the larger institutions," Lerner notes, "...and some of the younger, more entrepreneurial organizations that frankly aren't even bothering to become nonprofits because the situation is so grim"—will be well supported.

With total business giving to the arts representing roughly nine times the budget of the Arts' Endowment, corporate patronage warrants as much scrutiny as that federal agency has had to endure in recent years. There should be room in the

---

[28] Nina Kressner Cobb, *Looking Ahead: Private Sector Giving to the Arts and the Humanities* (Washington, DC: President's Committee on the Arts and the Humanities, 1995) 14.

[29] Robert Fitzpatrick, "Apocalypse Now and Then," keynote address, International Society of Performing Arts conference, New York, Dec. 18, 1996. A transcript of Fitzpatrick's remarks are available on ISPA's Web site (http://www.ispa-online.org/ispaconf/key-fitzpatrick.html).

corporate sector for the kind of merit-based funding that has more to do with rewarding arts organizations for a job well done, and less with how many new customers can be attracted through that kind of beneficence. New technology-based corporations, which benefit from the creative content of the arts, would be wise as well to invest in the nonprofit arts.

INDIVIDUALS: GIVING AND GETTING

Often overlooked in discussions of the arts infrastructure, which generally describe the transfer of funds from one institution (a foundation or corporation) to another (a museum or orchestra, for example), are the individuals who play key roles on both sides of that equation. In the arts as in all nonprofit fields, individuals collectively represent the single largest source of contributed income—over 80 percent of all charitable giving (and approaching 90 percent when individual bequests are added). No less important to the health of the field: the millions of hours of volunteer service that Americans contribute every year.

The picture of individual giving is a mixed one. Although five percent fewer households reported making contributions in 1995 than in 1993, the average contribution for all households (including non-contributors), after inflation, rose two percent, reversing a downward trend in such contributions that began in 1989. (For the 68.5 percent of households that reported contributions in 1995, moreover, the average contribution increased nearly 10 percent from 1993, after inflation, reversing a four-year slide.) Volunteering, similarly, has experienced a slight upturn, from the 48 percent of adults who volunteered in 1993 to 49 percent in 1995, but it was still down from the 54 percent who volunteered in 1989. The amount and value of this free labor, in any case, some 20.3 billion hours valued at $201 billion in 1995, remain highly significant.

If the importance of individual patrons often gets lost in the shuffle of institutional statistics, the importance of individual artists threatens to disappear altogether. Thanks to the analysis of census data over the past 20 years, we now know much more about the employment and earnings of artists, some 1.67 million of them, than ever before. We can speak with some confidence, for example, of average yearly earnings (authors led the way in 1989, at $23,335), of median ages (painters/craftspersons were the oldest, at 40 for males and 39 for females), and under-employment (dancers were the least likely to work a full year, with the median number of weeks worked in that field reaching only 39).[30]

Yet in other, crucial respects, particularly with regard to the context of bringing artist and audience together, we know comparatively little. How, for example, does the poet find a publisher, and how, in turn, does the literary magazine or the "small press" find an audience for that work? How does the composer find an ensemble to perform a new composition, and how does that ensemble, in turn, find a performance space or a record label to make that work more widely available? What happens to all of the independent films and videos that are made every year, some of which may find outlets on public television, but the vast majority of which are consigned to occasional screenings at media arts centers and museums?

In the popular marketplace, of course, it is hardly necessary to ask these questions, and the answers, in any case, are as close as the nearest Waldenbooks, Tower Records, or Blockbuster Video. The nonprofit sector, in contrast, offers up a treasure hunt for which few Americans are equipped with maps. Largely unaware of the cultural treasures that the existing production and distribution systems have managed to hide so effectively, the majority of Americans are not even likely to look very hard.

Most of the maps of the cultural terrain that we do have, moreover, are much more effective at charting the institutional landscape, although a handful of American Canvas participants urged the consideration of individual voices as well. Roberto Bedoya, executive director of the National Association of Artists' Organizations (representing some 350 artist-run organizations across the country), used his position as a member of the American Canvas Steering Committee both to underscore the importance of the individual artist to American culture, and to advise against losing sight of the artist's needs in our preoccupation with institutional growth. "America is experiencing a boom in the development of large cultural facilities—new libraries, museums, and concert halls," Bedoya observed. "Concurrently, significant capital improvement of existing cultural facilities is also occurring. In the face of all these millions being spent on arts institutions, artists are being told that there is less or no money for them."

---

[30] *Artists in the Workforce: Employment and Earnings, 1970-1990.*

Bedoya traces this curious dichotomy to our preference for "cultural illustrations over cultural inquiries…The importance of art in our society cannot be reduced to mean, 'If I have a museum I have art,' and in that process erase artists and their needs. All the talk about supporting our cultural infrastructure is worthless if we fail to support the essence of creativity—artists, their explorations, and inquiries."

AMERICANS AND THE ARTS

"I think our greatest failure," Barbara Nicholson declared at the American Canvas forum in Columbus, "has been that we have allowed the arts to be put into a little black box. The reality is that there is not a person…, whether they recognize it or not, that did not make some artistic decisions from the time they opened their eyes as they moved through the day."

Nicholson, director of the Martin Luther King, Jr., Performing and Cultural Arts Complex in Columbus, raised a theme that resonated throughout the six American Canvas forums. In enshrining art within the temples of culture—the museum, the concert hall, the proscenium stage—we may have lost touch with the *spirit* of art: its direct relevance to our lives. In building an intricate network of public and private support, the thousands of institutions over the past four decades, we may have stressed the specialized, professional aspects of the arts at the expense of their more pervasive, participatory nature. In the process, art became something that we watch other people do, usually highly skilled professionals, rather than something we do ourselves. "We may have nipped off the very grass roots of support that we need now," conceded Henry Moran, executive director of the Mid-America Arts Alliance at the San Antonio forum, "and that may have come about from our fascination with the role of institutions within the cultural ecology."

Institutions, after all, raise the money, sell the tickets, send out the press packets, present the art and generally squeak the loudest when the wheels of culture need lubrication. And they're the source of civic pride—the buildings that adorn the covers of chamber of commerce pamphlets, the festivals that are touted in tourist brochures. They're where we take the in-laws when they come to town for a visit. We're proud of these arts institutions, and for good reason.

But those same institutions may be obscuring our vision of the essence of art, too, the one-to-one relationship with the creative process that all Americans, whether they realize it or not, have every day of their lives. "I've never been in a home that didn't have art in it…," observed Steven Lavine, president of the California Institute of the Arts, at the Los Angeles forum. "…[But] a lot of people…have the experience of having been told by the appearance of what we used to call the 'elite organizations,' that what they are engaged in isn't the arts."

This process begins when we are very young, according to William Wilson, a folklorist at Brigham Young University and a participant in the Salt Lake City forum. Recalling his own personal background—coming from a family of railroaders, with childhood memories full of story telling, singing, and holiday feasts—Wilson noted that for all of their creative aspects, these activities never earned the mantle of art. "Through all of the years of my public education," Wilson recounted, "no teacher ever suggested to me that what I had experienced in my family…was of any artistic worth. Art was something we read about in books, not a crucial part of our own lives."

A half-continent away, and rooted in traditions even further afield, Gerald Yoshitomi faced very much the same homogenizing influence as a youngster. "I remember as a child growing up," the director of the Japanese American Cultural and Community Center recalled at the Los Angeles forum, "…there [were] a lot of Japanese-American arts around me day to day, and in my home was Japanese art…But as I went to school and I was educated, I was told that wasn't art. Art was something done by someone else. By another culture basically.…"

That failure to help our children make the connection between the expressive activities in the home, and the admittedly more formal, professional cultural traditions that may (or may not) have been included in the curriculum, is one that costs us dearly. The childhood experiences of Wilson and Yoshitomi, by no means rare, are symptomatic of the "black-box" compartmentalization of American culture. In treating art as essentially special and separate, we've failed to develop a vital link between the classroom and the home, one that could only enhance the educational process. So, too, have we failed to make a connection between participation and appreciation, between active involvement in our culture and the more passive spectatorship, prevalent in children's media especially, that threatens to undermine that culture.

"AN ESSENTIAL PART OF THE LIVES OF MOST FAMILIES"

Curiously, we tend to draw no such distinctions in the world of athletics, in which a direct connection is made between shooting baskets in the driveway and the professional exploits of a Michael Jordan, between jogging through the park and the world-class competition of the Olympic Games. Participation in such endeavors obviously means something to Americans, who spend over $50 billion annually on sporting goods. More than 110 million Americans attend professional baseball, basketball, and football every year (with an additional 72 million attending college football and basketball), and the connection between amateur activities and professional athletics is a real, mutually reinforcing, one. The 37 percent of Americans who attend spectator sports are more than matched by the 39 percent who play sports themselves.[1]

Shift from athletics to aesthetics, though, and the lines between participant and spectator are attenuated, if not severed altogether. Actually, many more Americans attend arts activities than professional sporting events every year, and considerable numbers participate even more directly—playing classical music (4 percent of the adult population in 1992), painting (10 percent), taking photographs (12 percent), or participating in modern dance (8 percent), creative writing (7 percent), or needlework (25 percent). Nevertheless, it cannot be claimed that the arts are in any meaningful sense integrated into our daily lives in quite the same way that sports are (which is why no less than 12 of the 25 highest rated television shows of all time were sporting events). And therein lies a lost opportunity, as a number of American Canvas participants pointed out, to enrich the lives of millions of Americans.

But first those walls that separate Americans from the arts will have to come down. "…If we really hope to strengthen families through the arts," William Wilson observed in Salt Lake City,

[1] National Endowment for the Arts, *Public Participation in the Arts, 1982-1992* (Washington, DC)

we must move away from the notion that art can only be found on the museum wall, at the concert hall, or on the performing stage. We must understand that art includes the expressive behaviors of ordinary people, like my railroader relatives, as they respond creatively to the circumstances of everyday life. If we will look, we will find art all around us—in the things that we make with our words (songs, stories, rhymes, proverbs), with our hands (quilts, knitting, raw-hide braiding, pie-crust designs, dinner-table arrangements, garden layouts) and with our actions (birthday and holiday celebrations, worship practice, playtime activities, work practices)...

Viewed in this light, Wilson continued, art "...is not something that exists 'out there' in a world alien to many families but is rather an essential part of the lives of most families. The problem is that they just don't know it."

Convincing Americans of the importance of the arts to their lives emerged as a new emphasis of arts advocacy at the American Canvas forums, joining more traditional emphases—in the legislative and civic arenas—as a basic message that the arts community must deliver. "Somehow," as Barbara Nicholson observed at the Columbus forum, "we have got to get back to the real definitions of what the arts truly are, so that we are not always in a position of having to justify or defend, but that everybody recognizes how important they are to their life."

For Wilson, that process must begin in the home: "If we want to help families through the arts, we must help them recognize, nourish, and value the art they already possess. As they begin to recognize the artistic merit of their own creative efforts, they may discover also the creative power of those art worlds that once seemed so foreign."

When Americans finally acknowledge the art that affects their own lives, the art in which they take an active part—in fashion and foodways, in song and celebration and stories—they'll be better prepared to commit to a public culture—the art and artists and arts organizations that labor in the nonprofit sector—with that same spirit of shared investment. Americans, to be sure, will continue to spend billions of dollars as more-or-less passive spectators of the entertainment industry ($5.5 billion on movies, $12.3 billion on recordings, and $19.5 billion on videos in 1995, for example). But they'll also be more sensitive, as "creators" themselves, to the needs of the aesthetic environment, and of the artists and arts organizations,

PHOTO BY JOHN BURRISON

Traditional craft artists like potter Lanier Meadow are part of a
National Endowment for the Arts Research study, *The Changing Faces of Tradition*,
which reviews the state of the folk arts field.

far from the commercial marketplace, that contribute so significantly to that
environment.

Wilson was not alone in this call to adjust our focus on the arts, to shift
from the traditional spot-lit close-up of the exceptional and the virtuosic to a pano-
ramic view of art's near-ubiquitous, more utilitarian presence in our lives. For the
architect Ray Huff, speaking at the Rock Hill forum, the key element is design, "a
working aspect of our everyday experience," he insisted. "Design in the most essential
manner, from the most elemental to the more pervasive—the kitchen utensil, the door-
knob, the pen, the highway overpass, the public park—is ever-present in our lives."

"...A COMMUNITY THAT IS DEFINED BY ITS PROBLEMS"

The change that Wilson, Huff, and many other American Canvas participants
called for is more than shifting our attention from the extraordinary to the ubiqui-
tous. We need a reexamination of the very function of the arts, how they help us

express our values and aspirations. The arts reflect our diversity, and yet also bring us together. They encompass family activities and values, even as they occasionally venture into more difficult terrain, helping us confront the troublesome issues of our time. For some Americans, finally, artistic expression provides something that is simply unavailable anywhere else: a sense of self-worth in a world that too often makes that kind of personal accounting impossible.

At the San Antonio forum, The Reverend Tony Campbell, rector of St. James Episcopal Church in Houston's tough Third Ward, talked about that accounting. "It's a community that is defined by its problems—poverty, despair, and hopelessness," Campbell explained. "And I think what we often forget in life is that individuals just don't spring up by themselves, that individuals come out of a culture. They receive their identity from that particular culture. So in my community...the business of the [church] is to provide hope and a way to live."

The arts play an important role in providing that hope, Campbell pointed out. "We have 200 kids who are fighting the image that the Third Ward tries to stamp on their heads—of people who are nobodies in our society. They are given a counter image: that you are somebody, you can produce, that you do have a life...So art is critical. It's crucial. It is the way we understand ourselves: It's not who we have been, but who we are, and where we are going."

One of the projects that Campbell's kids have worked on is a large mural, an enormous display that began as an act of vandalism—drug-related graffiti created by local gangs—but which evolved into something quite different. "We worked with the Museum of Fine Arts in Houston," Campbell explained, "and instead of just painting over the mural, we left half of the mural to stand, and we painted another half of the mural with the kids in the community. And so we left standing two dramatic images within that community: one of hopelessness and death and despair, but the other one of hope and life and joy."

Even for those who don't have to face the rigors of Houston's Third Ward, the arts can provide a powerful means of expressing one's values and aspirations. "The arts tell us who we are," declares sculptor Mary Ann Mears, a member of the Maryland State Arts Council and a participant at the American canvas forum in Charlotte. "You discover who you are through participating, whether you're making things or experiencing other people's work...When I've worked with kids with art, it's always amazing to me what it brings out of them."

And how important is that? "To me," Mears adds, exaggerating only slightly, "it's my religion, it's a matter as important as absolutely everything, whether it's eating and sleeping and breathing, or loving and being loved. It's as important as all of those things."

"WE ARE ALL A PART OF SEVERAL DIFFERENT CULTURES..."

The arts also have the capacity, as a number of American Canvas participants pointed out, both to express our diversity, accenting what is unique in the many strands that make up the American cultural fabric, as well as to bring us together, offering a common ground on which individuals who would not otherwise interact can get to know one another. The rifts in American society may be as broad as the chasm that often seems to separate blacks from whites, or as fine as the ethnic and racial gradations that make up our cities—the 90 languages that are spoken in Los Angeles public schools, for example, or the 87 linguistic groups from which Filipino-Americans spring.

One way or another, these cultural differences affect all of us. "We are all a part of several different cultures and sub-cultures at once," observed Adora Dupree, a storyteller from Nashville who participated in the Columbus forum. "Our culture may be ethnic, religious, familial, related to the university we attended, based in our neighborhood, or based in a shared political or sociological belief system. The arts are what essentially give us access to or define what our cultural heritage is."

Unfortunately, the differences that Dupree describes are often the source of friction in American society. But the arts, as Ohio State Representative E. J. Thomas pointed out at the Columbus forum, can counter these abrasive, divisive, ultimately destructive tendencies. "I sincerely believe that the arts are like a magnet in our communities," Thomas declared, "pulling us as diverse groups and cultures together when otherwise we would be content with the comfort of our own familiar cultural territory. Art provides us a positive tool with which to overcome the dynamics in human nature that tend to keep us separated."

Or, as Roderick Sykes, director of St. Elmo's Village in Los Angeles, expressed it at the American Canvas forum in his city, art provides a common language in a polyglot world: "When you don't know the language, creativity cuts across all those barriers. It tears down walls, it includes everyone." Choreographer Lula Washington, another American Canvas panelist in Los Angeles, shared that view, marveling at art's abilities to "develop avenues of respect for who we are and what we do," its value in "bringing together people that would not ordinarily come together."

Washington, who grew up in Watts, was late in settling upon dance as her career choice. She was 22, in college and with a husband and daughter, when a dance teacher introduced her to the work of Alvin Ailey. "Before that," Washington told Jennifer Dunning of the *New York Times,* "I had no idea dancing was something that would be possible for me as a black person. I had never seen live dance. My family didn't have money." Her exposure to Ailey's company changed all that. "This is it," Washington thought at the time. "This is something possible for me."[2]

After earning a master's degree in dance at UCLA, followed by commercial work in film, television, and stage shows, Washington founded the Los Angeles Contemporary Dance Theatre in 1980. Seventeen years later, that company, now known as the Lula Washington Dance Theatre, divides its time between national tours and community outreach, between creating ambitious new works that reflect the black experience in America and teaching children the basics of movement. Washington sees no conflict between the two activities. "When I was growing up," she explained to the *Los Angeles Times,* "I never had the opportunity to study dance. So, as I started to grow and develop, [working with children] became part of what I wanted to do with my dancing."[3] Thus the company's activities include an after-school dance, drumming, and gymnastics program for teen-agers called "I Do Dance, Not Drugs." Although the demands of community service can be physically and emotionally draining, particularly in gang-ravaged central-city Los Angeles, Washington has no regrets.

"I've never been in a home that didn't have art in it,

but a lot of people have the experience of having been

told...that what they are engaged in isn't the arts."

STEVEN LAVINE, CALIFORNIA INSTITUTE OF THE ARTS

---

[2] Jennifer Dunning, "Remembering Watts And, in the Process, Reaching to the Sky," *New York Times* 31 Aug. 1996.
[3] Jan Breslauer, "Dancing on Eggshells," *Los Angeles Times* 22 Oct. 1995.

She draws inspiration from the circumstances of her community for such works as "This Little Light," based on the life and struggles of Harriet Tubman; "Check This Out," a response to the 1992 LA riots; and "What About Watts?" a meditation on the gang violence that claimed the life of her own nephew in 1993 at the age of 13. Less than a year later, tragedy struck again, this time in the form of an earthquake that did some $800,000 worth of damage in her studio, housed in a 69-year-old former Masonic Temple. But for all of that, Washington's spirit remains indomitable. "My work is never dark," she explains. "It's always uplifting."

"...ARTISTS PLAYING THEIR TRADITIONAL ROLE OF TELLING THE TRUTH"

Washington's vision, and her use of dance to address social problems, are inspirational, and yet it's equally clear that art itself can occasionally be a problem. Or at least art, as the subject of contention and controversy, raises problems for some Americans. From the coarse lyrics of a popular musical group that sells millions of recordings, to the work of an obscure performance artist whose audience may number in the hundreds, art often finds itself at the center of controversy. Ever since the furor that broke out over the photography of Andres Serrano and Robert Mapplethorpe in 1989, scarcely a month has gone by in which the art world was not visited by one storm or another. Some of these tempests were more of the teapot variety, certainly, having much more to do with the immediate demands of a re-election campaign, and with the shallow, often manipulative nature of the mass media, than with legitimate differences of aesthetic opinion. These were political squabbles, in other words, masquerading as cultural debates, and serving neither politics nor culture in the process. That these disputes exist at all says something about the power of art, about the role of the artist in our society, and about the perceptions of Americans of the artists in their midst.

Steven Lavine addressed the topic of controversy and the arts at the Los Angeles forum, suggesting that the real question is not why the 90s have been so full of artistic controversies, but rather how we largely escaped such conflicts in the 70s and 80s. "We've gone through a fundamental generational change in what's going on in the arts," the president of the California Institute for the Arts explained. "The authority of a lot of old traditions wore away in the course of the 50s and 60s. We have an emergence in American culture where actually the most important voices are coming from places and cultures we didn't hear before. And, in fact, it does directly assault…what lots of the country would like to tell itself about the country. I don't know how we escaped the problem, because, in fact, it's the artists playing their traditional role of telling the truth. And people not wanting to hear it."

Artists, to be sure, will continue to raise issues and address topics that many of us, in a more perfect world, might not want to hear. The point is neither to dismiss such artists as malcontents, nor to punish them for making us feel uncomfortable, but rather to judge their work on its merits (or lack thereof) within a setting as free as possible from the vagaries of politics, and as full as practicable with the historical, social, and cultural context from which such art emanates. That's the approach taken by the Southeastern Center for Contemporary Art (SECCA) of Winston-Salem, NC, whose director, Susan Lubowsky Talbott, attended the American Canvas forum in Rock Hill, South Carolina.[4]

"Controversies surrounding the presentation of challenging art cannot be avoided," Talbott declared, "but it's possible to work with the community to resolve these issues." Among the solutions that SECCA has found is a program entitled "Artist and the Community," a series of three-week to three-month residencies that focus on issues critical to the Winston-Salem area, and which result in the creation and exhibition of new work. Working with other community-based institutions, moreover, the program is designed to forge a link between artists and a diverse range of community members. "As a participant in the 'culture wars,'" a museum statement reads,

> SECCA was also concerned with creating programs aimed at re-establishing bonds between artist, community, and cultural institution. If SECCA was to survive as a viable and valuable art and community center, it needed to mediate these conflicts on a local level. Winston-Salem could be a testing ground for a new kind of public art—one that could promote productive social change while introducing challenging new art forms to the community. Emphasis would be on collaboration and understanding rather than on the 'in-your-face' stance that previously characterized much public and political art.

[4] SECCA was awarded a grant over a number of years to support its Awards in the Visual Arts Series. It was this exhibition of a number of emerging photographers, including Andres Serrano, that touched off the political controversy of 1989.

During the course of developing this program in 1992 and 1993, museum staff researched issues that were of importance to the local community, identified artists with a strong record of community involvement, and located community groups representing culture, education, social service, and industry to serve as potential project partners. The museum initiated discussions with a number of community organizations, many of which had no history of collaborating with SECCA, and met as well with the local arts council and the mayor's office.

The result of this extensive planning has been a series of residencies and exhibitions that have earned both critical and popular acclaim. In 1994, installation artist Donald Lipski fabricated his work, "Oral Histories," largely out of tobacco products, in deference to the staple crop of the region, while Tim Rollins and K.O.S. (Kids of Survival) mounted *The Red Badge of Courage—Winston-Salem, North Carolina,*" involving 15 students from the Drop Out Prevention Program at Petree Middle School and Independence High School. The third project that year, Fred Wilson's "Insight: In Site: Incite: Memory," investigated the history of slavery in the Moravian community that founded Winston-Salem. Wilson's work, a multimedia installation in a historic house and a nineteenth-century black church (unused since 1950), proved so popular that it attracted national funding for a re-installation in 1995. Subsequent Artist and the Community projects involved artists working with local students, teachers, and a wide range of community members whose previous experience with formal arts institutions had been limited, and the project continues this year and next with Maya Lin working with area youth on an outdoor garden piece for Winston Lake Park, in a predominantly African-American neighborhood, and Iñigo Manglano-Ovalle's project that will address the concerns of Latino migrant farmworkers in the Winston-Salem area.

All of these projects reflect a museum that has managed to transform itself over the past several years, from "an institution under a great deal of attack because of Serrano," explains Talbott," to an institution that has been getting a great deal of support." It's not that the museum has steered clear of controversial works (which probably cannot be avoided in any case), but whenever the potential for controversy comes up, Talbott and her staff have sought input from the community itself in order to defuse the more explosive issues. She cites the "Civil Right Now" exhibition, which the museum presented two years ago, as a turning point for SECCA in its relations with the community.

"On the face of it, you wouldn't think this would be a terribly controversial exhibition," Talbott concedes, "but the curator of the exhibition felt that it was

COURTESY CITY OF ROCK HILL

The town of Rock Hill, South Carolina is graced by this statue of Civitas, which has become a civic emblem for this community which played host to an American Canvas Forum.

critical to include gay civil rights as well as racial civil rights, and some of the work in the show, for a small southern community like Winston-Salem, was a little bit 'edgy,' and we felt could be potentially controversial. Rather than censor the work out of the show, we took another tactic." That tactic included a special showing for a range of community leaders, black and white, conservative and liberal, whom Talbott had personally invited. "I called 40 of them, and I invited them to a special preview of the exhibition for a select group of community leaders, the point of which was to introduce them to the exhibition and to get their feedback on how they felt we should present the exhibition—so that it would be a working session, not just a tour, ...their reason for being there was to talk to us about their feelings about the exhibition, and help us strategize how to present this to the community. Suddenly, these people were all partners rather than adversaries." The result was a frank discussion of a number of works, including Serrano's photographs of the Ku

Klux Klan, and a debate over the inclusion of gay activists with civil rights leaders of the past. "At a fair amount of expense," Talbott notes, "…we re-did all of our explanatory panels…to say why this show was inclusive of so many ideas. The fact that we acted on their suggestions made a huge difference to the community."

Deborah Smith, director of the newly restored Opera House in Newberry, SC, and a participant in the Rock Hill forum, agreed that the context in which art is presented is extremely important, both for challenging work of the sort that SECCA presents, as well as for any newer material with which a local audience might not be familiar. Armed with the proper background information with which to approach such work, she believed, an audience stands a better chance of viewing art on its own terms, meeting the artist half way, as it were. Such "educative interchange" informed by both the artist's and the community's perspective, Chairman Jane Alexander added at the Rock Hill forum, "can be handled in a manner that does not vitiate the integrity of the artist or the institution involved."

"…OUR COMMUNITY IS ENGAGED IN A COLLABORATIVE IMPROVISATION"

Perhaps the final word on what the arts mean to Americans should go to Phillip Kent Bimstein, a participant in the American Canvas forum in Salt Lake City. "Some activists choose to spread their message through arts or music, others delve into politics," writes Andrew Kiraly in the *Las Vegas New Times.* "Phillip Kent Bimstein does both." First as a composer, and then as an arts council volunteer, and most recently as the mayor of a small town, Springdale, Utah, Bimstein has had three vantage points from which to view the arts.

As a composer and performer, Bimstein's career has zig-zagged all the way from the Chicago Conservatory of Music, where he majored in theory and composition, to "Phil 'n' the Blanks," a new wave rock group that released several recordings and music videos in the early 1980s. Following graduate studies in music at UCLA, Bimstein eventually settled in rural Utah, which provided the inspiration for what has become his most famous work to date, and something of an underground hit (although this being experimental, electronic music, it was pretty far underground). "I awoke one morning to the sounds of cows mooing in the pasture next to my home," Bimstein recalls. "Music to my ears, the moos became the inspiration for a concerto…*Garland Hirschi's Cows,* which premiered at the Salt Lake Alternative Music Festival in October 1990. The piece, which uses an Akai sampler to make music of the moos, also includes the voice of the cows' owner, Garland C. Hirschi of Rockville, Utah, as he tells the story of growing up with cows and what makes them moo."

Aside from the subject matter, however, this is not the kind of work one would suspect to emerge from bucolic, rural Utah, and as such probably owes as much to Bimstein's formal training in Chicago as it does to his new surroundings. But music has played an important role for Bimstein in Utah, too. "When I moved from Chicago to rural southern Utah eight years ago," Bimstein notes, "I didn't know a soul. Some of my old friends thought I would always be an outsider, but I was welcomed into the community. The vehicle that introduced me to my new neighbors, and which allowed me to get to know them, was my music." And the region continues to provide a rich vein of material for Bimstein's musical explorations.

Like a lot of modern composers, Bimstein works in a variety of styles, some more accessible than others, including works rooted in the history of his new surroundings in Utah. "I composed a work about the history of the area for the local church choir. At rehearsals I was warmly received, even though I am not a member of the church. At the 4th of July premier my wife sang in the choir, my parents drove in from California, and most of the town was there. I knew then that Springdale had truly become my home."

Bimstein's art eventually led him to the civic arena, initially as a member of the local arts council, and later in his effort to rally the community around the idea of presenting a contemporary music festival, the esteemed New Music Across America Festival, which included Springdale among 15 much larger cities in 1992. "For several years," Bimstein explains, "I served on the board of our local arts council. From that vantage point I saw our town transformed by the arts. Springdale had become fractured and polarized, divided by growth and development issues. People had lost respect and trust for each other, and were losing faith in our ability to get along. Town council meetings were hostile environments, and citizens hated to go. Our dialogue had broken down." With Vaclav Havel as his inspiration and using his position with the arts council as an entry point, Bimstein proposed a creative solution to the town's problems. "Our arts council presented a series of round-table discussions, entitled 'Embracing Opposites, In Search of the Public Good,' which helped us to develop a language of cooperation. Poetry readings, creativity workshops, and concerts became our positive meeting places, where we strengthened our social bonds, sustained our spirit, and nurtured the health back into our community. The arts provided the breeding ground for the cooperation and communication which brought us back together."

The arts also turned out to be the breeding ground for Bimstein's latest performance, as the mayor of Springdale. "That really surprised me," Bimstein admitted in an interview with the *Chicago Tribune,* speaking of his entry into local politics. "…[but] I realized that instead of regarding political office as a conflict with my life as a creative person, it could actually be a different manifestation of my creative side."

"The arts help me be a better mayor," Bimstein adds, "furnishing me with techniques which strengthen the bonds of our community. As a composer, I know that dissonant notes have value, and that even opposites can be orchestrated together. From a musical perspective, our community is engaged in a collaborative improvisation. If we play it well, a good work emerges, a constantly evolving composition."

CULTURE AND COMMUNITY

"The problem of the 20th century," W.E.B. Du Bois observed in 1900, "is the problem of the color line." Nearly a hundred years later, it cannot be said that the color line has been erased. On the contrary, that single line has evolved into a veritable grid, delimiting all manner of race and ethnicity, language and religion, social status and sexual orientation. Americans have grown accustomed to drawing lines everywhere, with English-only laws, welfare limitations, "three-strikes-and-your-out" sanctions, and a spate of referenda targeting affirmative action, gay rights, and immigration all designed to set the record straight. To make things right again. As if things ever really were right, and as if drawing yet another line would actually serve that purpose in any case.

The arts have not been free of such controversies, which have manifested themselves in a variety of forms, for both good and ill. On the positive side of the ledger, generations of artists, from the Harlem Renaissance in the 20s through the Civil Rights era of the 60s up to the most recent work of the Urban Bush Women and the Nuyorican Poets have added immeasurably to our cultural legacy. At the same time, the arts community has long labored under a stubbornly persistent class system of its own, one that continues to haunt the field: the recognition, palpable even in our democratic protestations to the contrary, that the audience for the non-profit arts remains highly skewed, betraying a demographic profile that tends to be older, wealthier, better educated, and whiter than a typical cross-section of the American public. Defenders of the field, understandably, point proudly to the progress that has been made in this regard—the 45 percent increase in the number of blacks who attended a live performance between 1982 and 1992, or the 64 percent increase in Asian, Latino, and Native attendance. But these figures, subsumed under categories that are largely class-based themselves, have as much to do with the cultural apartheid in which we began this century as they do with the cultural equality that, for all our efforts, remains as elusive as social, economic, and educational equality.

The difficult questions of equity and access, of opportunity and aspiration, are as critical to the future of American culture as they are to other aspects of American life. Although cultural equity and access were scheduled to be addressed at the final American Canvas forum in Miami, such issues, by their very nature, don't always wait for formal introductions. They initially came up in Columbus, not surprisingly, the very first stop on the American Canvas tour, and they literally boiled over in Los Angeles. The theme of that second meeting—How can the arts build and maintain the viability of a community's social infrastructure?—soon gave way to more pressing concerns, about race and class, inclusion and exclusion. Everything from the racial composition of the American Canvas panels themselves to the formality of the panelists' attire—"There's a cultural war going on," one audience member declared, "You don't dress up like this to fight a war!"—came up at various, often unscheduled, points during the two-day meeting. But it was Alberto Duron, Los Angeles attorney and cultural activist, who expressed the matter most succinctly.

"The arts can't help to ensure livable communities for tomorrow unless the arts establishment undergoes a wholesale overhaul," he flatly declared. "From the teachers, schools and student bodies in art schools, to the staffs at art museum and performing arts centers, and the gallery system, all these institutions must be opened up to the communities which they now claim to serve but don't."

Now claim to serve but don't: the phrase fairly crystallizes the bind in which the nonprofit arts often find themselves, as much the victims of their own institutional histories, and of the larger patterns of social and economic segregation, as they are complicit in these inequities. Duron, in any event, traced the arts community's recent woes, its political problems in general and its losses at the federal level in particular, to its failure to serve a larger public. "What's happened to public arts funding is in no small measure the fault of the arts institutions and the individuals who run them," Duron asserted. "Critics in Congress and elsewhere would never have been able to galvanize large segments of the public if it were not for the vulnerability of the arts community brought on by its isolation and intransigence." And until it addresses its own failings, Duron added, the arts community will be powerless to effect any real change in the larger society. Until arts institutions begin to forge closer ties with the communities around them, in other words, they will remain largely irrelevant, just so much costume jewelry on a body politic that has its mind on other, more pressing, concerns.

"Large segments of the community," Duron complained, "are ignored or showcased on a once-in-a-decade cycle. Community advisory groups are generally expected to be rubber stamps for institutional plans. Innovative ideas from these groups are generally ignored or quashed as uneconomical or outside of the institution's purview." In particular, Duron expressed grave reservations about the "Mexico: Thirty Centuries of Splendor" exhibition of 1990, typical of the touring "blockbuster" shows that steamroll through a city, drawing large crowds and stimulating vast sums of tourist expenditures, but otherwise doing little for local art and artists. And in this particular case, according to Duron, the sizable local Chicano community felt not only excluded from the event, but unnecessarily "exoticized" as well. "When it appeared in New York," Duron recalled, "the exhibition was highlighted as something foreign—'Come see something exotic'—and for the over three million Mexican-Americans who live in Los Angeles, we didn't want to be considered as something exotic."

The problem, Duron made clear, was not so much with the local venue for the exhibition (the Los Angeles County Museum of Art), as it was with the sponsorship of the Mexican government, whose diplomatic agenda had little to do with local interests and concerns. "As we kept telling them," Duron noted, "'After the carnival is over, we're going to be left behind here, and we're the ones who have to live with the consequences of you putting us forth as something exotic and strange and alien.' And that's exactly what we're trying to fight—the notion that we're somehow alien to this culture and this community."

As a result, the local arts community in Los Angeles rallied around an arts festival of its own, one that demonstrated, in reflecting the true diversity of the community and admitting participation from all sides, what a well-orchestrated arts event can really mean to a community. Spread over four months in 1991 and presented in a wide range of venues throughout the Los Angeles metropolitan area, the Artes de Mexico Festival attracted some 500,000 people to more than 230 visual arts, dance, theater, music, and poetry events. "Two years in the planning," Duron explained, "Artes was conceived as an opportunity for the entire Chicano artistic community to participate in a community-wide festival...." Festival organizers attempted to tap the rich vein of Chicano culture that had gone largely unnoticed by the area's major arts institutions over the previous 25 years. "We were continual-ly amazed at the high level of applicants wishing to become a part of the festival," Duron recalled. "...The artistic community—all of it—felt a sense of ownership and pride in being able to participate freely and without arbitrary constraints. The community responded by enthusiastically receiving the works and sharing in that same sense of ownership and pride."

"...THOSE NEW AUDIENCES THAT WE ALL TALK ABOUT AND CRAVE"

Duron's complaints, while timely, are unfortunately not new. They reflect long-standing concerns regarding the nonprofit arts' institutional relations with their communities, concerns that have troubled arts administrators for years. Over a decade ago, for example, at the aptly titled "Challenge of Change" conference in New York, the issue was addressed by Ruby Lerner, among others. "If we honestly assess our organizations," Lerner told the gathering of theater and dance profession-als in 1986, "we must conclude that their role is not integral to the lives of our communities; they are not true centers of our communities." Lerner, who had recently left the position of executive director of Alternate ROOTS (Regional Organization of Theaters South), was questioning, in effect, the degree to which the "Gotham City Ballet" or the "Metropolis Philharmonic" have any real connec-tions to either of those cities, beyond the use of their names. "What we have culti-vated to date," Lerner suggested, "some of us more successfully than others, are relationships with individuals of relative wealth (audiences and boards), dead indi-viduals of wealth (foundations), and the business community."

That audience-board-funder triumvirate has traditionally been a precari-ously narrow slice of American society, and the source of much consternation among an arts community that is determined to extend its reach beyond the aging audience base of traditional arts supporters. And yet financially speaking, at least, the arts community has long been sustained by its ties to institutional wealth and elite audiences. "These relationships," Lerner added, before asking the final, ironic question that continues to puzzle arts administrators to this day, "are motivated by our very real monetary needs. But I wonder if our close alignment with this small

Square dancing at the Bethel Youth Fiddle Camp in Pennsylvania
is one example of keeping folk traditions alive.

but powerful sector of the community may have limited and skewed what our organizations might become—in fact, may have been partly responsible for keeping away from our doors those new audiences that we all talk about and crave."[1]

The barriers that Lerner describes are subtle ones, and they don't show up very often in the lists of reasons survey respondents give for not attending arts events more often (where "not enough time" for city dwellers and "too far to go" for rural Americans are most likely to be cited). These barriers, moreover, are rooted in larger socio-economic factors—poverty, segregation, and illiteracy among them—that arts organizations alone are powerless to change. But that doesn't mean that growing numbers of them aren't trying. In a mountain-to-Mohammed shift that has no precedent in American culture (outside of wartime mobilization, perhaps), heretofore mainstream arts organizations have turned to a variety of social-

[1] *The Challenge of Change: Papers and Presentations from the 15th National Conference* (New York: FEDAPT, 1987) 112.

service and community-outreach programs. In the process, the distance between the arts institution and the settlement house, once situated on opposite sides of the tracks and even further apart philosophically, has shrunk considerably. Both are determined to prove their usefulness. Arts organizations have undergone this transformation, moreover, not only as a means of reaching "those new audiences that we all talk about and crave," as Lerner expressed it, but also, quite simply, as a means of survival.

"THE ARTS HAVE TO GO TO OTHER PLACES…"

Raising the issue of survival is not to suggest, as some critics have, that arts organizations have seized upon community activism for the same reason that Willie Sutton robbed banks—because that's where the money is. It is undeniable that funders, in the private sector especially, are increasingly looking for social justification for the grants they make. Everyone—grantors and grantees alike—are interested in reaching more people. "A theme for the future is to really decentralize what we are doing," explained Aldolfo Nodal, general manager of the Los Angeles Department of Cultural Affairs, at the American Canvas forum in his city, "…making sure that it goes out everywhere…. The arts have to go to other places…. We are starting to use some of the infrastructure that's already there, like the library system, the educational system…the police department…." Such nonarts agencies (and there are many more that could be added) are increasingly seen as the natural allies of the nonprofit arts community in its efforts to counter the exclusivity that Duron, Lerner, and others have cited.

"I would argue," writes William E. Strickland, Jr., executive director of the Manchester Craftsmen's Guild in Pittsburgh, "that the arts are a legitimate province of the many; that the best chance we have to rebuild broad based support for the arts and address the substantial social ills confronting our nation, is to recognize the arts have everything to do with daily life and with all people in every community in our nation." Ironically, the arts community could learn a lot in this regard, Strickland suggests, from some of the smaller cultural tributaries, indigenous and immigrant alike, that the mainstream institutions have tended to overlook in the past. "The traditions of Native American, Appalachian White, African American and Hispanic cultures," he points out, "clearly illustrate the close relationship that culture plays in daily life. Craft, dancing, storytelling and song are intrinsic elements of life within these ethnic groups. I believe the arts have a special opportunity to go beyond 'art for arts sake' and embrace the reality of art for life's sake."[2]

Clearly, much has changed in the ten years since Lerner, who now directs the Association of Independent Video and Filmmakers, raised the issue. Many more arts organizations—looking and acting less like the traditional institutional structures to which Lerner was referring in 1986—have established roots that are beginning to spread more evenly throughout the communities in which they operate. They are accomplishing this in a number of ways—if not, in fact, by expanding their traditional audience base, then by inserting the arts into a variety of social and civic contexts well beyond the aesthetic realm to which the arts community has traditionally confined itself.

Perhaps it's simply a matter of historical timing: social activism among artists ran high in the 1930s and the 1960s, when economic and political events, along with general social unrest, proved to be stimulating influences. And the 1990s, while not nearly as turbulent as these earlier periods, offer plenty of targets for the socially-minded artist, especially as the public sector retreats from its erstwhile social responsibilities, leaving in tatters that "safety net" that many Americans had once taken for granted. It's too early to assess the new cultural activism of the 1990s (although that hasn't prevented some critics from laying the decline of western civilization at the door of arts organizations that work with the poor and the afflicted), but the movement in general seems less political and more utilitarian than its earlier incarnations. Again, without doubting for an instant the sincerity of arts organizations that endeavor to contribute to the social welfare, there is also more than a trace of desperation—the recognition that ours is not a society that places a sufficiently high value on the arts to support them for their aesthetic contributions alone—in some of the arts activism of the 90s.

This new pragmatism accepts the need to "translate" the value of the arts into more general civic, social, and educational terms that will be more readily understood, by the general public and by their elected officials alike. That theme was especially prominent at the American Canvas forum in Rock Hill, which provided a handy lexicon for the artist or arts administrator desiring to speak the new

[2] Quoted in Grady Hillman, *Artists in the Community: Training Artists to Work in Alternative Settings* (Washington, DC, Americans for the Arts: 1996) 4.

language of arts activism in America. For Ben Boozer, executive director of the South Carolina Downtown Development Association, the key term was economic development, and the role that the arts play therein.

"The arts are like seeds planted in our community.

With minimal attention, the seeds will grow. But with

---

nurturing, they will grow and bear fruit for the whole

---

community."

MICHAEL HIGHTOWER, *PRESIDENT*, NATIONAL ASSOCIATION OF COUNTIES

The role that culture plays in the local economy is likely to become more prevalent as basic, bottom-line considerations continue to capture the nation's imagination. Betty Jo Rhea, the mayor of Rock Hill, spoke more generally of the quality-of-life factor, and the contributions of the arts in making a city more attractive, both to the general public as well as to the business community. William Simms, president of Transamerica Reinsurance and former chairman of the Charlotte/Mecklenburg Arts & Science Council referred to as a city's "feel-good element that makes people want to be there, makes businesses want to relocate there, encourages business to grow." A number of panelists, meanwhile, stressed the educational aspects of the arts, both formally, as an essential ingredient in the basic K-12 curriculum, as well as more generally in the need to serve the cultural interests of all Americans. Kathy deNobriga, executive director of Alternate ROOTS, put the entire matter more bluntly: we need to find a way to translate what is "obvious to us—the importance of the arts—into terms that politicians will understand."

"WE MUST FIND THE LINE ITEMS...THE DOLLAR SIGNS..."

Questions of vocabulary aside, the real issue, according to Syd Blackmarr, president of the Georgia Assembly of Community Arts Agencies, is as much where these conversations take place as it is precisely how they are couched. Long accustomed to talking among themselves, the arts community must now begin to carry its conversations beyond its own narrow borders, Blackmarr insisted, getting more involved in civic affairs, for example, by joining planning boards and other "tables of power."

"It is time for those who know the power of the arts," Blackmarr urged, "to become members of the school board, the city and county commission, the planning and zoning commission, the housing authority, the merchants association, the library board." The point is not simply to underscore the relevance of the arts to these various civic concerns, but to tap the public funds that flow through these channels, some of which might be used for the arts. "We must insist that when roads, sewers, prisons, libraries and schools are planned and funded," Blackmarr explained, "that the arts are also planned and funded. We must find the line items, the budget categories, the dollar signs in all of these local sources; and then insist that the arts receive their fair share as a vital and essential element of commerce, education, community identity, cohesiveness and development. Traditional funding sources should encourage and reward unique collaborations between the arts and every possible community partnership which leads to growth of the true spirit of community."

Mary Ann Mears, a Baltimore-based sculptor and a member of the Maryland State Arts Council, cited a number of agencies in the public sector—the Departments of Commerce, Housing and Urban Development, and the Small Business Administration in particular—that warranted input from artists. At the Columbus forum, Anna White of Young Audiences of Indiana had made very much the same point concerning the need to expand opportunities for the arts to play a larger role in community affairs. "Artists, arts administrators and those who support the arts can no longer exist in isolation," White insisted. "It is time to bring to the table various segments of the community—religious, philanthropic, civic, business and the arts in a way that will utilize the creative thinking and energy that is the basis of all artistic endeavor, to join in the endeavor to reform our schools, to rejuvenate our neighborhoods and to re-instill in our people a sense of civic responsibility and pride."

There was much talk at the several American Canvas meetings about the extent to which the arts community often operates in relative isolation, off in a corner somewhere, away from those tables where the key decisions are made. "Sometimes you can't always expect the people to come to our table," concluded choreographer Lula Washington at the Los Angeles forum. "We have to go to their table."

"...THE FASTEST GROWING PROGRAM...OF LOCAL ARTS AGENCIES"

To the extent that this artist-as-citizen vision is being realized today, it's happening at the level of local government, especially within the universe of local arts agencies (LAAs), which are increasingly turning to the kind of "communitarian," civic concerns that lend themselves to collective action. A recent study of LAAs in the nation's 50 largest cities, in fact, reveals a universal acceptance of the premise that the arts can and must play a direct role in community affairs. "Using the arts to address community development issues," the report notes, "...continues to be the fastest growing program and service area of local arts agencies. 100 percent of LAAs in the 50 largest U.S. cities use the arts to address community development issues, an increase from 88 percent in 1994 and approximately 20 percent in 1986."[3]

In addition to the traditional activities undertaken by LAAs (cultural programming, grantmaking, services to artists and arts organizations, and community cultural planning), growing numbers of them, often in partnership with the arts organizations they support, are venturing into a broad range of community-based activities. In 1996, fully two-thirds of the 50 largest LAAs addressed five or more of the issues listed below:[4]

COMMUNITY DEVELOPMENT ISSUES	% OF LAAS INVOLVED
Cultural/Racial Awareness	93%
Youth at Risk	88%
Economic Development	76%
Crime Prevention	63%
Illiteracy	56%
AIDS	51%
Environment	51%
Substance Abuse	46%
Housing	44%
Teen Pregnancy	41%
Homelessness	34%

[3] National Assembly of Local Arts Agencies, "United States Urban Arts Federation: A Report on the Arts Councils in the 50 Largest U.S. Cities," June 1996, 7.
[4] National Assembly of Local Arts Agencies, "United States Urban Arts Federation" 7.

Equally important, LAAs are increasingly working with other community organizations and agencies in order to undertake these activities. All but one of the 50 largest LAAs reported involvement with one or more of the partnerships listed below:[5]

COLLABORATION AND PARTNERSHIPS	% OF LAAS INVOLVED
Neighborhood/community organizations	81%
School districts	76%
Parks and recreation department	73%
Convention or visitor's bureau	56%
Economic development department	51%
Chamber of Commerce	44%
Housing	39%
Social service departments	39%
Library	37%
Law enforcement	27%
Other	12%

Perhaps most notably for the nonprofit arts, a sector that must have despaired of ever again seeing economic charts that didn't slope downward, the record of local government support for the 50 largest LAAs is refreshingly up-beat—a total 35.3 increase since 1990. Although only a tiny fraction of the nearly four thousand LAAs across the land, those 50 largest LAAs represent a healthy slice—32 percent—of local arts funding overall. Equally important, while budgets elsewhere wither, support for the arts at the local level shows surprising strength.

Americans for the Arts (AFA), having changed its name from the National Assembly of Local Arts Agencies after merging with the American Council on the Arts last year, continues to lead the way in helping arts organizations integrate their activities into community affairs. AFA's Institute for Community Development and the Arts, now in its third year of operation, serves as a clearinghouse of information and ideas in this area, having examined more than 650 community arts programs nationwide in its first year of operation alone, with a goal of researching and documenting a thousand programs in the institute's "Arts Answers Database."

[5] National Assembly of Local Arts Agencies, "United States Urban Arts Federation" 9.

In its commitment to sharing information as broadly as possible, the institute has published a number of important studies, including *Building America's Communities: A Compendium of Arts and Community Development Programs; Resource Development Handbook: Untapped Public Funding for the Arts; Working Relationships: The Arts, Education and Community Development; The Arts Build Communities: A Training Handbook on Arts Programming* and *Public Housing; and Artists in the Community: Training Artists to Work in Alternative Settings.* Collectively, these several studies represent an invaluable guide to the integration of the arts into civic and community affairs, at once tapping the expertise of those in the field who have long worked in these areas, as well as pointing the way to future directions that are likely to be increasingly important to the arts.

Among those new directions is an effort to reclaim and expand the shrinking "public space" for civic dialogue in this country, where a broad range of social and cultural issues—including the future of the nonprofit arts—can be discussed in an environment tainted neither by the hypocrisy of partisan politics nor the triviality of the mass media. Thus AFA is undertaking, in conjunction with the Ford Foundation, a project entitled "Expanding the Civic Role of the Arts: The Arts and Civic Dialogue." Having assembled a diverse team of advisors and engaged the services of the noted theater performer Anna Deavere Smith, the project is off to a promising start.

"...THE SOURCE OF A POSITIVE, LASTING IMPRESSION..."

While there are no one-size-fits-all models for the integration of the arts into community life, two areas in particular—urban revitalization and cultural tourism—are especially popular right now, and both were the subject of much attention at the American Canvas forums. In many respects, of course, revitalization and tourism are simply two sides of the same coin: as cities become more "livable" and more attractive, they'll prove increasingly alluring to tourists, whose expenditures, in turn, will help revitalize cities. As mutually reinforcing pieces of the same puzzle, moreover, both urban revitalization and cultural tourism invite the participation of arts organizations. The arts can come to these particular "tables," in other words, confident that they won't be turned away.

"The tourism industry and the arts community," observed Ilene D. Kamsler of the Colorado Hotel and Lodging Association at the American Canvas forum in

PHOTO BY ED CROCKER

CORNERSTONES Community Partnership is an initiative in New Mexico
that helps people plan and restore historic adobe churches,
including this one in the town of Pajarito.

San Antonio, "share in a unique symbiotic relationship that unfortunately is not clearly recognized by either entity. As 'cultural tourism' becomes more institutionalized,
tourist destinations rely on the promotion of indigenous culture and arts to attract
visitors." Speaking on behalf of the tourism industry at the Columbus forum,
Michael J. Wilson, president of the Greater Cincinnati Convention and Visitors
Bureau, offered some insight into the keenly competitive nature of his field, and the
pivotal role the arts can play in that competition: "As one can well imagine, the marketing of destinations all across the country is an extremely competitive industry;
and to remain successful, one must aggressively promote those features and attributes
that create an advantage over the competition. To that extent, the arts represent a
tremendous asset to these sales efforts, recognizing that all forms of art—creative,
performing, musical, architectural, etcetera —contribute to the essence and unique-

ness of each of our communities. In many cases a destination's image, perception, or identity is largely based upon some aspect of the arts in that respective area."

"In cities where the arts flourish," Wilson continued, "there is a distinct understanding and appreciation of their contribution to the community's quality of life and economic vitality. This understanding fosters civic participation—not as an obligation, but as a matter of choice." As an example of this cultural and civic synergy, Wilson cited his own city of Cincinnati, where the new downtown Aronoff Center for the Arts "was completed as a result of investments made by the state of Ohio, local corporations, and area-wide individuals. This arts center has played an essential role in revitalizing much of our downtown area with investments in new businesses, increased spending, and steady activity that brings people back to the downtown for entertainment purposes."

A recent study conducted by the Travel Industry Association of America substantiates Wilson's views. As America's favorite tourist attractions, museums ranked third (behind shopping and outdoor activities) and cultural events ranked sixth (trailing beaches and parks), well ahead of sports, gambling, nightlife, and amusement parks.[6] "To those of us directly involved in destination marketing," Wilson concluded, "it remains clear that the arts, and all they embody, are an essential ingredient in the mix of features that accentuate a community's uniqueness as a visitor destination. They are often the source of a positive, lasting impression that attracts visitors back to our cities time and time again."

But as the American Canvas participants were quick to point out, it is not simply the tourist population that benefits from vibrant cultural districts. The local residents are also well served by these developments, too, a fact that Victoria Hamilton, executive director of San Diego's Commission for Arts and Culture, underscored at the Los Angeles forum. "Local arts agencies have become community change agents," Hamilton asserted,

> *by using the arts as a community development tool. By partnering with artists and arts organizations local arts agencies have contributed to the vitality of a city. The development of these public/private partnerships have proven to be a cost-effective way to meet the challenges facing urban America on many levels. Investment in culture has brought tremendous*

---

[6] Edwin McDowell, "Tourists Respond To Lure of Culture," *New York Times* 24 Apr. 1997: D1.

economic benefit to American cities. There is no other city contracted ser-vice that collectively impacts business, tourism, the development of livable communities and the quality of life for citizens.

"...A SITUATION WHERE WE CANNOT SUCCEED"

That belief in the power of art to change communities is not one necessarily shared by the majority of Americans, however. Arts organizations cannot afford to assume that their community-development efforts will prove any more popular than, say, the arts events they produce, in which public non-participation rates in seven distinct areas range anywhere from 73 percent to 96 percent.[7] In a 1994 survey of public confidence levels in various public and private institutions, "arts, culture, and humanities organizations" did not fare particularly well. Less than a third of those surveyed (29.3 percent) expressed either "a great deal" or "quite a lot" of confidence in these organizations, which finished thirteenth out of 23 institutional categories (thirteenth out of only 19 categories when those inveterate doormats, political and governmental organizations, are excluded from the list). Twelve percent of the people surveyed were simply unaware of what cultural organizations do, apparently, in either their arts- or their community-related activities.[8]

Nor can arts organizations afford to assume that in their new role as "catalysts for change and renewal," they'll be any more successful than the failed (and/or curtailed) public-sector social-service programs that saddled the arts—among other sectors—with the burden of becoming social problem-solvers in the first place. When the arts find themselves valued primarily for their purely utilitarian aspects, many observers become troubled.

"All of a sudden," as Ruby Lerner has expressed it, "the arts are valuable if they can solve social problems, and of course, God knows we couldn't solve social problems in the social arena, but now it's expected that in the cultural arena we'll be able to solve all these problems—'and, by the way, we won't be able to give you many resources to do this.' So, I think this is completely unrealistic, and it is setting us up to fail...." Some organizations, Lerner concedes, are well suited (if not equally well supported) to continue their work in the social arena, but she sees trouble ahead for other organizations, caught up in the communitarian spirit of the

[7] *Survey of Public Participation in the Arts, 1982-1992.*
[8] Virginia Hodgkinson, Murray Weitzman, and the Gallup Organization, Inc., *Giving & Volunteering in the United States: 1994 Edition* (Washington, DC: The Independent Sector, 1994).

times, or simply running out of other options, that turn to social work as a means of staying afloat. "The organizations that have a history of doing that work should be well supported," she believes, "much better supported that they've been historically, to do that work. But I think that for organizations that have not been doing that work, to twist themselves around now into some shape so that they can do that work—maybe not even very well—is self-defeating. I have a lot of reservations about that…. We're putting ourselves into a situation where we cannot succeed."

It would be a mistake to assume, however, (which Lerner would be the first to acknowledge), that the arts world cleaves neatly between those organizations that venture into the "real world," determined to fight crime, poverty, racism, and substance abuse, and those that remain behind, tending solely to the vineyards of aesthetics. As Phyllis Brzozowska reminded us at the Columbus forum, sounding a theme that echoed through each of the subsequent regional forums, the connection between art and "everyday life" is a vital one: "…There are so many ways that art is in our everyday life," explained Brzozowska, whose Dayton Stories Project aims to bring the art of storytelling to bear on local concerns. "It is not just on the concert stage and in the theater in a way that you have to pay money for, although those are wonderful. But it is when people connect with the art in their everyday life that they can really value the art we put up on the stage.…"

ARTS AND EDUCATION

"It was the best of times, it was the worst of times," proclaimed Charles Dickens in *A Tale of Two Cities*, raising ambivalence to new literary heights. Curiously, Dickens's uncertain description of revolutionary-era Paris is an apt one for the current state of public education in the United States, where rising expectations battle declining test scores for space on the front pages of the nation's newspapers. Curiouser still, it is precisely *because* these are the worst of times, with more pressure than ever before on our schools to pull themselves out of a prolonged downward spiral, that these are also potentially the best of times for arts education. Since nothing else has worked, the arts and humanities are poised to become leading contenders in the school-reform sweepstakes and to re-establish themselves in the basic K-12 curriculum.

Many Americans over the age of 40, ironically, can recall a time when the arts were a part of that curriculum. Routinely during the first half of this century, students received at least a smattering of arts education, and many received much more than that. If the arts were never part of the "3 Rs," various assortments of music, drama, painting, and crafts were a regular part of the school curriculum for many years. Eventually, specialists in music and the visual arts were assigned to schools, and field trips to museums and symphony orchestras (later facilitated by Young Audiences and similar nonprofit organizations) were common. However uneven their implementation across the country, the arts at least had a place in most children's schooling.

The first significant setback for the arts came with the heightened emphasis on science and math following the launch of Sputnik in 1957, when the country, nervous about its standing in the Cold War, asked a generation of students to "buckle down." That ominous phrase didn't automatically signal an end to arts education, but more often than not, when school boards enumerated the "frills" that might be sacrificed in the interests of competing with the Soviets, the arts were among the first to go.

Conversely, just a few years later, the pendulum began to swing back in the other direction, with the establishment of the Arts and Humanities Endowments in 1965. Among those offering testimony on behalf of the new program, for example, was Glenn T. Seaborg, chairman of the U.S. Atomic Energy Commission. "If we are to achieve humanity in terms of its greatest fulfillment, we need to share deeply in the varied experience that can be reached only through the arts and humane letters."[1]

Equally important was the passage that same year of the Elementary and Secondary Education Act, Title III of which pumped millions of dollars into public schools for a variety of curricular innovations, including cultural enrichment programs. But these were three-year funds, for add-on programs. Thus despite the flurry of activity in the 60s, 70s and 80s—a period in which artists-in-the-schools programs proliferated, when alliances between schools and arts organizations flourished, and when an advocacy movement rallied around the often competing causes of hands-on arts training, exposure to practicing artists, and systematic instruction in the history, theory, and criticism of various "high art" traditions—the arts did not have a secure place in the basic curriculum.

"Every child is an artist. The problem is how to remain an artist once he grows up."

PABLO PICASSO

---

[1] U.S. Congress, Senate, National Arts and Humanities Foundations. Hearings before the Special Subcommittee on Arts and Humanities of the Committee on Labor and Public Welfare, 89th Cong., 1st Sess. (1969) pt. 2, 404.

A variety of factors, actually, have conspired against arts education in recent years. At the top of everyone's list, obviously, are budget constraints. When it became necessary for school districts to cut back on their offerings to students, arts programs were often included in the list of dispensable items. But other pressures played a role, too, including the need to accommodate a much more diverse, and constantly evolving, student population, one that often required increased attention to basic language and other remedial skills. The curriculum itself, in other words, has taken on new concerns over the years, reflecting social, economic, and psychological issues directly related to the complex times in which we live. A lot more has changed than the one-room schoolhouse itself in the long history of public education in this country. Life outside that schoolhouse has changed radically, too, and our curricular values have shifted accordingly.

"THE ARTS ARE A DEFINITE PART OF THE TURN-AROUND PROCESS"

The arts' tenuous relationship with our schools was a major part of the American Canvas inquiry. If there was one thing on which all participants in the American Canvas could agree, in fact, it was the importance of arts in the classroom, not simply for the arts community, but also for the public at large. Although only the forum in Salt Lake City was intended to address educational issues specifically, the topic came up again and again at all of the meetings. The arts, both as subject matters themselves, and as an enhancement of other areas of the curriculum, were regarded as central to a sound education. The arts are a natural way for children to learn a wide variety of subjects, Kendis Marcotte pointed out at the forum in Los Angeles. "They may not even know that they are learning grammar and spelling when they are writing a play...," explained the director of the Virginia Avenue Project, a theater that brings children together with professional artists to create original plays and build long-term mentoring relationships. "And even more than that, [the children learn] a creative way of thinking, a creative way of problem solving—a creative process that can be translated later into virtually any endeavor they go into."

In that connection, several forum participants cited the relevance of arts education to the findings of Department of Labor's Secretary's Commission on Achieving Necessary Skills (SCANS), in which the arts lend themselves to developing those cognitive, interpersonal, and strategic skills that are judged essential to success in the modern world.[2]

The value of the arts in nontraditional educational settings, especially in reaching those who have not succeeded in formal school programs in the past, was also noted at the forums, as were the arts' many contributions to family unity and growth. Speaking of the former issue in Los Angeles, Tom Stang of the Phoenix Academy, a part of the Phoenix House drug rehabilitation center, described the benefits of an arts-based curriculum in his work with troubled youth. "I have been in the classroom on a daily basis for 20 years," Stang explained, "and if there is one thing I have learned as a teacher, it is that the arts are the soul of the education program.

… The arts are a way of getting the students back on the education track. Some of them come to us as early as 12 or 13 years of age and stay for 14 to 18 months. In this time we are able to repair a lot of holes in their past education, give them the confidence necessary to feel success in an academic setting so they can continue their education at a regular public school when they graduate from the drug rehabilitation program. Some are now aspiring to enter the Los Angeles High School of the Arts at California State [University] Los Angeles or enroll in art programs at the college level when they leave us. This is a very positive legacy for students who come to us with nothing but a series of F grades on their report cards together with a lot of absenteeism. The arts are a definite part of the turn-around process.

"DO WE WONDER WHY THE ARTS ARE A LOW PRIORITY IN THE CURRICULUM?"

"The statistics on the number of arts specialists are appalling," reported Joan Boyett, vice president for education at the Music Center of Los Angeles, at the American Canvas forum in that city. "There are 45 million students, grades K-12, in the United States and more than 15,000 school districts. However, the responsibility for reinforcing the teaching of the arts at the district level rests in the

---

[2] U.S. Department of Labor, Secretary's Commission on Achieving Necessary Skills, *What Work Requires of Schools: A SCANS Report for America 2000* (Washington, DC: Department of Labor, 1991); *Learning a Living: A Blueprint for High Performance* (Washington, DC: Department of Labor, 1992.

hands of only 114 music supervisors and 59 art supervisors—nationwide. No separate figures are available for the number of theater or dance supervisors: is it possible that there are none? Do we wonder why the arts are a low priority in the curriculum?"

It is not for lack of trying that the arts have failed to establish a stronger foothold in the nation's schools, however, and several of the American Canvas participants described a number of existing programs that are working to ensure that the arts will enjoy a more central place in the nation's schools in the future. That's one of the objectives of the Goals 2000: Educate America Act, certainly, although the inclusion of the arts in that legislation was by no means a certainty when the reform process began in 1989. That was the year in which President Bush and the governors of the 50 states agreed on a set of "National Education Goals," including a call for all students to demonstrate competency in "challenging subject matter," namely, math, science, reading, writing, and geography. Conspicuous in its absence was any mention of the arts in the listing of core subjects, an oversight that was rectified only after considerable lobbying on the part of the arts and education community, which made a significant breakthrough.

That curriculum, in the final analysis, reflects social values, and the arts, for better or worse, have not always fared so well in that regard. The landmark *Nation at Risk* report of 1983, for example, signaling the start of an educational reform movement that continues, in one form or another, to this day, did not even mention the arts.[3] Neither a part of the problem nor, apparently, a viable solution either, arts education had become more a matter of local circumstance than of national consensus. Fortunate were the students in those school districts that employed specialists in the arts, or in those schools that maintained working relationships with local arts organizations, or in those classrooms in which the teacher, perhaps recalling her own experience as a child, insisted that the arts be a part of the basic curriculum. But overall, the situation was grim, as the Arts Endowment made clear in *Toward Civilization,* its 1988 report on arts education: "The arts are in triple jeopardy: they are not viewed as serious; knowledge itself is not

[3] National Commission on Excellence in Education, *A Nation at Risk* (Washington, DC: Department of Education, 1983).

viewed as a prime educational objective; and those who determine school curricula do not agree on what arts education is."[4]

If that analysis found the low point for arts education in this country, the picture has improved markedly in several respects since then, including a much clearer sense of "what arts education is." Internecine battles pitting proponents of "discipline-based arts education" (encompassing art production, history, criticism, and aesthetics) against those who favored less rigorous "arts exposure" programs have largely subsided, with more interest today in tending to the larger task of ensuring that the arts assume their rightful place within the basic K-12 curriculum. Arts education, according to the National Coalition for Education in the Arts, should be defined broadly, as "the process of teaching and learning how to create and produce the visual and performing arts and how to understand and evaluate art forms created by others." At a minimum, according to this consortium of 28 national arts organizations, the ideal curriculum "encompasses four basic aspects with the expectation that students will:

~ Create and perform the arts;
~ Understand the role and importance of the arts in culture and history;
~ Perceive and respond to the qualities of the arts; and
~ Make sound judgments about the arts and understand the bases upon which those judgments rest."[5]

Admittedly, that definition does little to address the other two parts of arts education's "triple jeopardy"—the perception of the arts as electives rather than as essentials, and the more recent preoccupation with making schools "safe and order-ly"—but progress is being made on these fronts, too.

"...THE TRANSFORMING POWERS OF THE ARTS"

In addition to developments within the private sector—of which the work of the Getty Education Institute for the Arts is among the most significant—arts education has made strides in the public-policy arena as well.[6] First, in 1992, former Secretary of Education Lamar Alexander established the America 2000 Arts Education Partnership

---

[4] *Toward Civilization* 19.
[5] Arts Education Partnership Working Group, *The Power of the Arts to Transform Education* (Washington, DC: John F. Kennedy Center for the Arts, 1993) 5.

in conjunction with the National Endowment for the Arts, charged with recommending ways to integrate the arts into the larger educational reform movement. The Partnership's Working Group, co-chaired by James Wolfenson, then chairman of the Kennedy Center, and Harold Williams of the J. Paul Getty Trust, issued *The Power of the Arts to Transform Education,* a 1993 report that helped solidify the arts' claim to an array of benefits for students, teachers, and the general "learning environment" alike. "Experienced observers tell us, and data increasingly support claims," the report declared, "that schools with strong arts programs regularly incur such benefits as:

- ~ Intensified student motivation to learn;
- ~ Better attendance among students and teachers;
- ~ Increased graduation rates;
- ~ Improved multicultural understanding;
- ~ Renewed and invigorated faculty;
- ~ More highly engaged students (which traditional approaches fail to inspire);
- ~ Development of a higher order of thinking skills, creativity, and problem-solving ability; and
- ~ Greater community participation and support.

The report concluded:

> *The arts contribute to an overall culture of excellence in a school. They are an effective means of connecting children to each other and helping them gain an understanding of the creators who preceded them. They provide schools with a ready way to formulate relationships across and among traditional disciplines and to connect ideas and notice patterns. Works of art provide effective means for linking information in history and social studies, mathematics, science, and geography. A work of art can lead to many related areas of learning, opening lines of inquiry, revealing that art, like life, is lived in a complex world not easily defined in discrete subjects.*[7]

[6] See. for example, Elliot W. Eisner, *The Role of Discipline-Based Education in America's Schools* (Los Angeles: Getty Center for Education in the Arts, 1988); *Discipline-Based Arts Education and Cultural Diversity: Seminar Proceedings,* August 6-9, 1992, Austin, Texas (Los Angeles: Getty Center for Education in the Arts, 1993); *Perspectives on Education Reform: Arts Education as Catalyst* (Los Angeles: Getty Center for Education in the Arts, 1993).

[7] *The Power of the Arts to Transform Education* 7.

More significantly, the working group's recommendations managed to find a home in the legislation that was soon proposed by the new secretary of education, Richard Riley, as the arts became one of the core subjects in the Goals 2000 legislation, and the working group's sense of "the transforming powers of the arts" was incorporated into the Improving America's Schools Act, reauthorization legislation for the Elementary and Secondary Education Act.

The field has also found success in the area of assessing the proficiencies of students in various basic subjects. The National Assessment of Educational Progress, popularly known as "The Nation's Report Card," had not included the arts within its analysis for over two decades. But in the Spring of 1997, at selected eighth-grade sites, student proficiencies have been measured in dance, music, theater, and the visual arts. The NAEP "Report Card" on what American eight-graders know and can do in the arts will be released by the Department of Education in May, 1998. Eventually, using standards developed by a consortium of national associations in arts education and supported by the Department of Education and the arts and humanities endowments, student competency in the arts will be routinely measured at the completion of grades 4, 8, and 12.

The National Standards for Arts Education stipulate that, by the time they have completed secondary school, students should be able to:

~ *Communicate at a basic level in the four arts disciplines*—dance, music, theatre, and the visual arts. This includes knowledge and skills in the use of the basic vocabularies, materials, tools, techniques, and intellectual methods of each arts discipline.

~ *Communicate proficiently in at least one art form,* including the ability to define and solve artistic problems with insight, reason, and technical proficiency.

~ *Develop and present basic analyses of works of art* from structural, historical, and cultural perspectives, and from combinations of those perspectives.

~ *Have an informed acquaintance with exemplary works of art* from a variety of cultures and historical periods, and a basic understanding of historical development in the arts disciplines, across the arts , and within cultures.

~ *Relate various types of knowledge and skills within and across the arts disciplines.* This includes mixing and matching competencies and understanding in art-making, history and culture, and analysis in any arts-related project.

"As a result," the standards conclude, "students can arrive at their own knowledge, beliefs, and values for making personal and artistic decisions. In other terms, they can arrive at a broad-based, well-grounded understanding of the nature, value, and meaning of the arts as a part of their own humanity."[8]

"...THE ARTS ARE INDISPENSABLE TO EDUCATION REFORM"

Such standards, in the arts as in all other areas of the K-12 curriculum, are voluntary, and they may be supplemented or modified by content standards developed by some states or ignored entirely by others. And just as a partnership effort was required to get to the point at which the arts are "on the table" of educational reform, so will keeping the arts at the forefront of that reform movement demand a similarly united effort. That's one of the reasons Secretary Riley and Chairman Jane Alexander convened the planning group that produced *The Arts and Education: Partners in Achieving Our National Education Goals,* an action plan subsequently endorsed by representatives from more than 100 national organizations in the fall of 1994. The report offered the clearest rationale to date for the importance of the arts to a sound education. "Three broad arguments—cultural, educational, and economic—about the value and power of the arts for education serve as the foundation for an argument for their integral part in helping our children achieve challenging education goals and high standards:

> *As part of the heritage of our culture, the arts are forms of understanding that are fundamental to what it means to be an educated person. They are the richest and most far-reaching expressions of human creativity, achievement and communication—from people to people, culture to culture, and age to age. To lack an education in the arts is to be profoundly disconnected from our history, from beauty, from other cultures, and from other forms of expression. The arts are basic, as well, to securing a humane future for our children....*

---

[8] Consortium of National Arts Education Associations, Dance, Music, Theatre, Visual Arts: *What Every Young American Should Know and Be Able to Do in the Arts* (Reston, VA: Music Educators National Conference) 18-19.

"More particular to the educational aims of the Goals 2000: Educate America Act," the report continues, "the arts are indispensable to education reform. The very idea that we can change our schools and make them more effective centers of learning without educating children in the arts is simply false...." The report offers four reasons for placing the arts at the heart of the broader reform movement, citing the variety of ways that children learn (based on Howard Gardner's pioneering research into "multiple intelligences"), the range of analytical and problem-solving skills that students will have to master, the diversity of students that must be served by schools today (including those who have often been "disempowered and disenfranchised" in more traditional educational settings), and the connections that need to be made among the several academic areas themselves as well as among events and activities outside of the classroom.[9]

In light of those connections, especially, the economic implications of a sound arts education also become much clearer. "As part of their preparation for productive work," the Arts and Education report concludes, "the arts help students build the specific workplace skills needed to ensure their own employability and their ability to make a solid economic contribution to our communities and to the nation. The arts teach and enhance such skills as the ability to manage resources, the interpersonal skills of cooperation and teamwork, the ability to acquire and use information and to master different types of symbol systems, and the skills required to use a variety of technologies."[10]

The fall 1994 meeting of national organizations that endorsed this report also produced the Goals 2000 Arts Education Partnership, a Washington-based organization designed to implement the action plan and to facilitate communication and advocacy at the national, state, and local levels. This partnership of arts, education, business, advocacy, and funding organizations is administered by the Council of Chief State School Officers and the National Assembly of State Arts Agencies, through a cooperative agreement with the Arts Endowment and the Department of Education.

---

[9] Gardner identified seven distinct intelligences: musical, bodily-kinesthetic, logical-mathematical, linguistic, spacial, interpersonal, and intrapersonal. See Howard Gardner, *Frames of Mind: The Theory of Multiple Intelligences* (New York, Basic Books, 1983).

[10] *The Arts and Education: Partners in Achieving Our National Goals* (Washington, DC: National Endowment for the Arts, 1995) 21-22.

At Pyramid Atlantic in Maryland, community members
of all ages participate in arts programs designed to ensure that
creativity and imagination remain part of lifelong learning.

"THE ARTS... MUST BE POSITIONED AS EQUALLY 'TOUGH.'"

The director of that organization, Richard J. Deasy, participated in the American
Canvas forum in Salt Lake City, and he presented cogent arguments that the arts
community will have to marshal in its effort to ensure that arts education moves
beyond the good intentions of Goals 2000 and into the nation's classrooms.

"The fundamental problem we confront in making the arts an unques-
tioned part of the learning required of students and teachers," Deasy observed, "is
the position of the arts in the broader culture." No one at the American Canvas
forums, certainly, needed to be reminded of the losses the arts have sustained in the
political arena, and by extension in the public mind, in recent years; but even in
the absence of these setbacks, the arts have long suffered in comparison to other,
more valued aspects of American life. Deasy suggested the term "muscularity" as a

general description of what is most valued in America: "toughness (tough minded-ness, competitiveness, triumph over pain in its various forms), physical prowess as good itself and as a preferred means of settling affairs (war, violence, no-holds-barred argument) and, lately, muscular bodies as signs of health and equality. Success at work and life is thought to flow from this kind of toughness." Certain parts of the curriculum, Deasy pointed out, including math, science, reading and writing, are associated with that kind of toughness, as are sports programs among extracurricular activities. "Displacing these values is virtually impossible," Deasy conceded. "The arts, therefore, must be positioned as equally 'tough.' Toward this end the research evidence on the developments they produce in the growing brain and body of the child and young person should be continually documented and presented."

Recent research on the development of the brain demonstrates the power of training in music and other art forms to improve spatial reasoning and similar cognitive skills of the very young. Writing in the February 1997 issue of *Neurological Research,* psychologist Frances Rauscher of the University of Wisconsin at Oshkosh and physicist Gordon Shaw of the University of California at Irvine report that pre-schoolers who were given piano keyboard lessons scored 34 percent higher on tests measuring spatial-temporal ability (useful in math, science, and engineering) than did other preschoolers. Other researchers, as reported in the May 1996 issue of *Nature,* have demonstrated similarly positive effects of music training on young children. Concerning a group of first-graders in Pawtucket, Rhode Island, those children in the more active music program, the study found, per-formed significantly better in both math and reading.

Studies such as these, Deasy believes, should be more widely publicized, not the least because they have the cachet of "scientific research" attached to them. Yet as a recent Department of Education publication points out, there's also an ele-ment of common sense to these studies: "Children naturally sing, dance, draw and role-play in an effort to understand the world around them and communicate their thoughts about it. A growing body of evidence demonstrates that when their care-takers engage them in these activities early in life on a regular basis, they are help-ing to wire the children's brains for successful learning."[11]

---

[11] "Arts Education Contributes to Early Childhood Brain Development," *Community Update* (April 1997): 1.

"...THE BASIS OF SELF-ESTEEM THAT IS ESSENTIAL TO ALL LEARNING"

As in so many other conversations, then, especially those that take place in the civic and political realms, the value of the arts needs to be "translated" into terms that educators and parents understand. "The arts are all we say they are when we talk of profundity, joy, delight and inspiration," Deasy observes. "But these terms and perspectives do not render them 'muscular'; [the arts] are, therefore, wonderful but dispensable to those who manage the central cultural institution of our society: the school."

Making arts education "indispensable," Deasy argues, is a matter of demonstrating the importance of the arts—to all students—in terms that extend well beyond the intrinsic aesthetic qualities of the arts themselves. More than mere embellishments to the "real work" that schools have to carry out, the arts are a part of those basic tasks, and they require the same dedicated study that other parts of the basic curriculum demand. "Mastery of the arts," Deasy insists, "requires rigorous, substantive and disciplined study and practice of their forms, principles and methods–a study that demands and rewards excellence: the basis of self-esteem that is essential to all learning."

If these are the arguments that need to be made in order to ensure the inclusion of the arts in our schools, what are the conditions in which the arts will flourish in that setting? Deasy suggests four critical factors:

~ well-trained and skilled teachers and/or teaching artists who have a command of an arts discipline and/or a deep understanding of its forms, principles and methods and its history and tradition;

~ a well-designed and planned program that takes into account child and adolescent development and the multiple ways in which students learn;

~ an institutional and community belief in the value of the arts in education and stable policies and resources; (sustaining these beliefs, policies and resources requires a network of education, arts and cultural leaders and institutions orchestrated in support of arts in schools.)

~ an entity or institution external to the school, but linked to it, that develops knowledge through research and makes it available in meaningful ways to school personnel and decision makers. Entities can include a higher education institution, a research center, or an arts funder or institution with a substantial understanding of education. Long term commitment by these entities is essential.

"Efforts should focus on creating these conditions in every community," Deasy concludes. "Three sets of interlocking relationships should be fostered: systematic collaboration among the arts and cultural institutions, a formalized compact of cooperation between these collaborating institutions and the elementary and secondary education system, and a formalized arrangement between and among these sectors and the higher education/research institution or institutions. A nurturing of these relationships should be provided by governmental bodies and by the business and corporate sector."

"ACADEMICS + ARTS = ACHIEVEMENT"

Too often in the past, however, that "interlocking relationship" has been more of a house of cards, based largely on the desire of well meaning arts organizations to embark on educational ventures, and to generate additional earned and contributed income in the process by furnishing educational services to local schools. Much less evident in these alliances is the kind of thoroughgoing commitment, on the part of the schools themselves, that an arts education program requires if it is to succeed. Richard Bell, executive director of Young Audiences (which presented more than 60,000 arts programs to 6.5 million children through the U.S. in 1995) and a member of the American Canvas committee, has written of these old-style arts partnerships that, for all of their good intentions, generally failed to take root in the schools.

"Historically," Bell observes, "most arts partnerships have been designed from the perspective of individual arts organizations. For example, a symphony would form a partnership with several schools to bring students to the concert hall or a local arts-in-education program would join in partnership with a museum to create a visual arts residency." In most cases, Bell notes, these partnerships were built to specifications defined by the arts organizations rather than by the schools, with most funding coming from the private sector, and with project coordination, fiscal responsibility, and programmatic continuity vested in individuals outside of the school system itself. "The problem with these partnerships has not been a matter of artistic quality or effectiveness in meeting the goals set out for them," Bell concludes. "Rather, the goals have not fully met the needs of students and schools. No matter how well designed and executed these programs may be, providing worthwhile arts experiences for the benefit of a few students has suddenly become passé because there is little opportunity or motivation to integrate these programs into the general curriculum and school budgets."[12]

Ralph Burgard believes he has a better idea. He, too, is well aware of the hit-and-run programs that Bell described. "There have been, here and there," he concedes "some interesting efforts in arts education across the country, but I still tend to think of them as 'enhanced enrichment programs.' Basically, they are coming of necessity from the outside into the system. It's not the school system rushing out to embrace these programs, it's the insistent advocacy on the part of cultural institutions, with the assistance of individual artists, who try and infiltrate this huge bureaucracy and say 'pay attention to us, we are more valuable than you think.' By and large most school systems view those efforts as outside efforts."

Since 1987, Burgard has been working instead on the inside, helping to set up what he calls the "A+ School Program," which designates the program's basic approach: "Academics + Arts = Achievement." There are now 39 A+ schools operating in five states, all based on the same basic principles. First, the school faculty must vote to undertake, for a minimum of four years, a program of daily arts instruction and interdisciplinary teaching for all students in the school. Second, that instruction will consist of at least one full period of arts daily, covering at least four disciplines each week (usually visual arts, music, dance, theater, or media arts). Third, to meet this commitment, a sufficient number of arts teachers will be hired to fulfill the arts instruction duties. Fourth, all teachers will use interdisciplinary, hands-on instruction, where appropriate, to teach the course of study mandated by state and local education authorities. Interdisciplinary units, often based on particular themes, will be phased in over the first three years, using teams of classroom teachers. Fifth, participating schools are expected to develop strong, two-way partnerships with their communities and regions—with parents, with local cultural agencies and individual artists, with schools of education that train their teachers, and with the media. Sixth, these schools will participate in continuing staff and administration development, including a five-day summer institute before the program begins. Additional staff development workshops in each school throughout the year will further support the transition into more extensive interdisciplinary teaching, reflecting the different learning styles of both teachers and students.

---

[12] Richard Bell, "Building Continuity and Systemic Change: A Primer on the New Arts Partnerships," in *Beyond Enrichment: Building Effective Arts Partnerships With Schools and Your Community*, ed. Jane Remer (New York: ACA Books, 1996) 147.

PHOTO COURTESY THE HEARD MUSEUM

Children peek through a doorway of a Tsimshian longhouse,
native to the Pacific Northwest Coast, at the "Old Ways, New Ways"
exhibition at the Heard Museum in Phoenix, Arizona.

"I think that what has helped A+ more than anything else," Burgard
explains, "is the sense of teachers and administrators that this is an 'inside' program, because it is adding teachers to their roster everyday—full-time teachers—
and it starts in the classroom every single day, and then is supplemented, as it must
be, by those outside experiences that we've been trying to get in for so many years.
But essentially it starts first within the schools and in the school community...."
That "school community," Burgard adds, "is an enormously powerful and sometimes defensive unit because of all this [public] pressure, and they close ranks.
Anything that is new, there is a good percentage of teachers that will wait until it
goes away. They won't actively oppose it, but they just wait it out, and by and large
they always win."

By securing staff and faculty support before the program even begins, and
by learning what each school and community hope to accomplish, Burgard has
managed to find an environment conducive to his experiment in arts and education. "My feeling is that if we are trying to approach or...infiltrate a huge bureaucracy.... Once it's in, I have great confidence in the power, the eternal power, of the

arts to completely change and 'corrupt' the school building, the way we think it should be. But where we usually falter is in the process of getting in, and with most of the enrichment programs…the bulk of the money usually comes from outside sources. It's very seldom that a school board will put up the full funding or even 50 percent of it. So as a result, we are continually dashing around and trying to raise money for it."

Burgard has been much more successful with the funding of A+, earning commitments from both within the school system as well as from outside sources. In North Carolina, for example, where 27 schools are part of the program, the Kenan Institute for the Arts has been the primary sponsor since 1993. For the four-year evaluation period (1995-99), a number of foundations and corporations have joined in the funding, as has the North Carolina General Assembly, which provided $500,000 annually over the past two years. These state funds match the commitments by the school districts and their private funders, and if the program proves effective over the four-year evaluation period, it is expected that the schools will adopt A+ as their core education program and support it through their regular school budgets.

The evaluation, in addition to measuring academic achievement, will also assess other indicators of school improvement, including the level of satisfaction for students, parents, and teachers, the level of parent involvement, as well as changes in drop-out rates, attendance, and the need for disciplinary actions. The early returns, Burgard reports, are promising. After using the A+ Schools Program for just one year, Sunset Park Elementary School in Wilmington, NC, (a school with 84 percent of its students participating in the free and reduced-cost lunch program, and in which 62 percent of the students are minority) saw student disciplinary actions drop from 130 to 50 and suspensions from 32 to 3. At the end of the second year, writing tests administered by the state saw the fourth-grade students improve some 30 percentile points, jumping all the way from the 35th to the 65th percentile in a single year.

But academic improvement is only a part of the puzzle, Burgard points out. "Typically," he writes, "Americans ask their public schools to fulfill other missions as well as educate their children. Recent polls show that parents want their schools to be safe, orderly and productive. In effect, they want schools to become more vital communities where students acquire the social skills to work together and respect one another. The outcomes could strongly affect the nation's social, economic and educational health." Programs such as A+, he believes, can serve these very ends, reflecting the social and cultural functions that the arts have traditionally played. "For thousands of years," he points out, "the arts have provided shared experiences that bring people together in places of worship, weddings, festivals and other celebrations. When taught daily in American schools they can and are creating small and large communities of students and teachers in the classroom and throughout the school. By working in groups to prepare performances and exhibitions, students gain respect and appreciation for one another. They create what used to be called in simpler times 'school spirit,' a sense of shared purpose that is the basis for all vital communities."[13]

"A SURVIVAL IMPERATIVE IN OUR SOCIETY"

In simpler times, of course, our communities were in better shape, too, which is one of the reasons arts organizations have extended their educational activities into the community itself. The mere existence of an institution known as the "Museum of Tolerance" is suggestive of the larger educative role that the arts often play, and of their value in bridging some of the larger, more treacherous gaps that separate Americans from one another. Gerald Margolis, director of this Los Angeles-based museum, part of the Simon Weisenthal Center, participated in the Los Angeles forum, described the social and cultural pressures of that region. "Los Angeles exemplifies American diversity in microcosm," Gerald Margolis explained. "...From the Los Angeles Riots to the Simpson trial, intergroup tensions have rocked Southern California, unleashing centrifugal forces. The varied communities of Southern California need opportunities to speak—not at—but to each other. And alienated communities will never thrive unless they are reconnected and learn to live in harmony in our 'global village.'"

Margolis's museum has come up with a variety of means to promote that kind of harmony, such as "Investing in Diversity," a program that brought in 92,000 students last year alone. "This is a primary program of the museum that deals with incipient prejudices before they grow into ingrained hatreds," Margolis explained. Targeting older citizens, "Tools for Tolerance for Professionals" is an all-

---

[13] Ralph Burgard, *Schools as Communities: Public Education and Social Cohesion,* 1997.

day seminar in diversity issues for front-line service providers in the fields of education, social work, health care, and law enforcement. Reaching out more broadly
still, "Confronting the Nineties: Critical Issues in America" is a series of public
forums that has addressed such issues as media coverage of minorities, sexual
harassment in the workplace, the future of affirmative action, the First Amendment
in the electronic age, the educational needs of the physically challenged, women's
issues, and gay and lesbian rights. Film and exhibition programs, finally, further
incorporate the arts in the museum's efforts to serve the multiplicity of ethnic and
racial communities that make up Southern California.

"Both in its permanent hi-tech installation on tolerance in America and
the history of the Holocaust," Margolis elaborated, "as well as in the changing ex-
hibits program, the Museum of Tolerance addresses the multi-ethnic fabric of the
American Canvas, and how valuing diversity is no longer simply an ideal but a
survival imperative in our society. With all of its challenges and problems, Los
Angeles and Southern California will remain a testing ground for new possibilities
of social accord and understanding. The threat to this engagement will be in a
retreat into ethnic insularity, tribalism, and distrust. Art can move us beyond
boundaries by communicating on the commonalty of human experience and the
valuing of difference."

The Museum of Tolerance is just one of a growing number of cultural
organizations whose educational activities reach directly into the community.
More than 200 of these programs are profiled in *Coming Up Taller: Arts and
Humanities Programs for Children and Youth At-Risk,* by the President's Committee
on the Arts an the Humanities.[14] The Lied Discovery Children's Museum in Las
Vegas, for example, in response to the needs of its immediate neighborhood
(which is 59 percent minority, with over one-third of the households living below
the federal poverty line), has established arts programs to serve young people.
Suzanne LeBlanc, executive director of the museum and a participant at the
American Canvas forum in Salt Lake City, described one of those programs,
ArtSmarts. This program, she explained, "provides young people from 10 to 18,
particularly those in the community with the least access to artistic experiences

---

[14] Judith Humphreys Weitz, *Coming Up Taller: Arts and Humanities Programs for Children and Youth At Risk*
(Washington, DC: President's Committee on the Arts and the Humanities, 1996). See also Nancy Welch
and Paul Fisher, *Working Relationships: The Arts, Education and Community Development* (Washington,
DC: National Assembly of Local Arts Agencies, 1995).

and methods of expression, the opportunity to work alongside a professional artist for an extended period of time on a group art project. The artist and the participants work together to develop an idea, investigate different ways of carrying it out, and create a finished artwork or performance, which is presented to the public. ArtSmarts not only provides young people artistic training, but also gives them experience using the artistic process as a method of problem-solving and learning about oneself and the world at large."

With major support from the DeWitt Wallace-Reader's Digest Fund (part of its national YouthALIVE! initiative), ArtSmarts projects have included a large, portable mural based on Jacob Lawrence's Migration Series (with artist Dennis Angel), a documentary video entitled "Street Talk," (with filmmaker Amie Williams), and "Earthscapes," a performance piece based on local environmental issues (with dance and choreographer Maria Medina). "These projects have been incredible," says Sue Fink, ArtSmarts coordinator. "The kids involved have gotten a whole new perspective on how much hard work an artist puts into a project. They've also gotten a lot of terrific information about the many professions available to artists, like architecture, graphic arts, and teaching."

"...ART IS STILL AT THE TOP OF THE LIST FOR CUTTING..."

Arts education programs such as these, whether operating in the classroom or in the community at large, didn't come about without a considerable amount of effort, and they're unlikely to be sustained without equal amounts of advocacy. The basic message, concerning the importance of the arts to a sound education, has been promulgated widely at the national level in recent years, by the Arts Endowment and by Secretary of Education Riley among others. Yet that same message has not always been translated successfully at the state and local levels, where art is still at the top of the list for cutting in a budget crunch. Nor is it simply a matter of economics, Larry Williams, chairman of the executive board of the Western States Arts Foundation, pointed out in Salt Lake City. "You've never heard the school board sit and debate whether or not we're going to have mathematics in the curriculum." The debate over the inclusion of the arts won't be settled satisfactorily, he predicted, until we have a generation of graduates, themselves the beneficiaries of an education that includes the arts, who have entered society and assumed positions of leadership.

In the meantime, Gerald Yoshitomi pointed out at the Los Angeles forum, arts educators and their advocates will need to learn the same lesson that the larger arts community has learned in recent years, looking beyond the main streets of American culture to some of the less prominent thoroughfares. "There has been actually a growth, a tremendous growth in arts education for young people," the director of the Japanese American Cultural and Community Center observed, "…[but] it hasn't been in the public schools, and it hasn't been in western European forms. It's been in church basements, in ethnic cultural halls, and people's living rooms."

Regardless of the focus of arts education advocacy, whether it's the classroom, the community, or the church basement, the arguments marshaled on behalf of the arts will have to be carefully crafted. "Utilitarian arguments in support of the arts are understandable in these difficult, distrustful times," writes playwright and director Alan Brody, responding to the recent research on the positive effects of arts training on the development of a child's brain. "They serve as weapons in the political and ideological battles raging in the school districts of America, but they ultimately subvert the very meaning of art. In the end, that could prove even more dangerous than the loss of government support."

Brody worries that some of the handiest arguments of the moment, designed to convince skeptics of the value of the arts, may, in the long run, prove counter-productive. "Arguments that can serve up the arts as a teaching tool or a source of revenue are tempting expedients," he concedes. "But if we depend on those we may one day find ourselves making and teaching something that is not art at all, only something that helps students read and count—or someone else to get rich. The very thing we were hoping to protect will be once again held in contempt."

Brody, for one, has a happier ending in mind. Writing with the optimism that perhaps only an artist in the midst of a campus full of scientists and engineers can muster, the associate provost for the arts at the Massachusetts Institute for Technology looks forward to the next scientific study that underscores the importance of art: "If…we refind our voices and our faith in the necessity of artistic practice, if we are able once more to celebrate the lasting value of the journey into the human heart and imagination, then perhaps one day we will hear the news that researchers have shown how the study of reading and mathematics can make us all better artists."

THE ARTS AND TELECOMMUNICATIONS

Of all the social and economic forces that affect the nonprofit arts and audiences for the arts perhaps none is as perplexing as the swift development of telecommunications in the 90s. The high-tech hardware and software explosion—from multimedia to the so-called Information Superhighway—caught many nonprofits unprepared. We're invariably left grasping at virtual straws in our efforts to determine precisely what it is that has everyone talking. Will television sets become smarter, more interactive, or will computers become cheaper, more pervasive? Is it 500 channels of programming that's coming our way, or video-on-demand? What about the millions of pages on the World Wide Web? Are we headed toward a digital promised land, or simply, as some fear, a "vaster wasteland"?

Where, in any case, do the arts fit into these several versions of the future? Many in the arts community pin their hopes on a glorious new world of online multimedia—in which an endless variety of full-motion video, CD-quality sound, late-breaking news, and personalized information will one day stream into the nation's 100 million households via a broad-band network. For now, at least, that vision has turned out to be a zero-billion-dollar industry. Aside from a handful of advertising-supported Web sites, no one is making much money on the Internet. The money that is changing hands—an estimated $300-500 million in online advertising and sales transactions last year—may sound like a lot, but it's a small fraction of the $160 *billion* in advertising expenditures overall, or the $45 billion in traditional catalog sales. In the world of Big Business, at least, the Information Superhighway is still pretty much a country road.

Which is not to say it's not important—or that it won't prove increasingly so in the next century—to the lives of growing numbers of Americans. The role of technology in our lives—from the pervasiveness of television to the expansiveness of the Internet—has already begun to generate a backlash. Sven Birkerts and others worry about technology over-mediating our lives[1], and it is true that one of the problems with television and the Internet is that they take up a lot of our time. More time online means less time experiencing the arts live, and the arts community must find many ways to use technology to augment the current cultural landscape. There are too many important issues involved to simply ignore the impact of technology on the arts.

Generally silent during the crucial debate that preceded the passage of the Telecommunications Act of 1996, the arts community was largely denied a seat at the table during the policy formation. None of the Department of Commerce's several Information Infrastructure Task Force working groups included the arts within their sweep, and there was not a single representative of the nonprofit arts among the 37 members of the U.S. Advisory Council on the National Information Infrastructure. The Telecommunications Infrastructure and Information Assistance Program, it is true, has made funds available for cultural projects over the past four years, but the results have been meager. Of the 11 program areas that were funded in the initial three rounds, the arts and culture finished dead last, garnering less than three percent of the funds awarded. And while there are isolated pockets of technological savvy among the various cultural agencies in Washington—including the Library of Congress, the Smithsonian Institution, the National Gallery of Art, the National Endowment for the Humanities, and the National Endowment for the Arts—this sector has yet to collaborate in any meaningful sense.

For its part, the arts community has proved to be only slightly more resourceful in this area. With a handful of exceptions, including the Arts Wire network (a program of the New York Foundation of the Arts that dates from 1992),

---

[1] See Sven Birkerts, *The Gutenberg Elegies: The Fate of Reading in an Electronic Age* (Fawcett Books, 1995) and *Tolstoy's Dictaphone* (Graywolf Press, 1996).

and the collaborative National Initiative for a Networked Cultural Heritage (NINCH), the field has generally failed to work cooperatively in this area. NINCH, however, shows great promise. The Initiative began in 1993 as a collaborative project of the American Council of Learned Societies, the Coalition for Networked Information, and the Getty Information Institute (then known as the Getty Art History Information Program). "A diverse coalition of cultural organizations," according to its mission statement, "dedicated to ensuring the greatest participation of all parts of the cultural community in the digital environment…" NINCH's mission

> *is to advocate for the inclusion of the cultural sector in all policy deliberations on the future of the information infrastructure and to educate policymakers, coalition members and the general public about the critical importance of translating the vision of a connected, distributed and accessible collection of cultural knowledge into a working reality.*[2]

In one area, at least, the arts community has been remarkably active of late, establishing a colorful presence on the World Wide Web. However belated and fragmented that effort has been, there are literally thousands of pages given over to culture on the Web, from the largest museums to the smallest artists' spaces to individual artists of all stripes. The Web offers a semblance, at least, of the very attributes—participation, interactivity, collaboration—that are so conspicuously absent from the more traditional media. The Web has a tremendous amount to offer to the nonprofit arts sector—as a means of advertising its wares, of sharing information, and even, albeit in a fairly rudimentary fashion right now, of presenting creative work to new audiences.

What tends to be overlooked, however, in the understandable excitement surrounding ever-more elaborate, multimedia-laden Web sites, is that the WWW is an *application*, not a final destination. It's the top card—for now—on a deck (the Internet) that is expanding and evolving in a manner that even the most technologically astute, or financially shrewd, have difficulty grasping. One thing, at least, is

---

[2] From NINCH web site at www.ninch.cni.org

PHOTO COURTESY WGBH

In the studios of Boston's WGBH, Margot Stage narrates
a Descriptive Video Service script for *The American Experience*,
to provide narrative links to television programs for the blind.

certain: that what began as an essentially "public" venture, serving scientific, academic, and military interests, will become increasingly "private" in its character and direction, driven by corporate investment, shaped by market forces. Ironically, in the process, the online world under corporate control will reach infinitely more people, with a greater variety of services, than ever before. Certainly the tiny cadre of technological elites who connected to the Internet in its early years pales in comparison to the millions who surf the Web today, or the many millions over whom, in the future, the online waters will wash.

Still, the crucial distinction between public interest and private development holds, for that vast new "public" that will be digitally interconnected in the next century will have one vital characteristic in common: they'll all be customers. The electronic menus from which they'll make their selections, moreover, will reflect much more complex pricing models than today's flat-rate schemes, including premium services that only the wealthy will be able to afford. Commercial content, similarly, will push more specialized fare (including civic discourse and nonprofit culture) into the "slower lanes" and more obscure "neighborhoods" of the online world. Thus despite our tendency, in waxing eloquent on the promise of the digital future, to speak in terms of "digital town halls" and "electronic library cards", the reality, for most Americans, is likely to be much more mundane. If the current commercialization of the Internet is any indication, at least, there'll be far more virtual shopping malls and multiplex cinemas than town halls in our online future, the passport to which won't be the library card, but the credit card.

The real promise of the digital frontier is not the animated Yellow Pages of the World Wide Web, nor the commercial juggernaut that threatens to homogenize the online world in much the same way that it has stifled alternative voices in the existing mass media. Even if only at the margins, there will be room for alternatives to the mainstream entertainment, for more radical variations—departures, even—on the standard, bifurcated themes of creation and presentation, artist and audience, spectator and participant. We've grown accustomed, in reckoning the online future, to think solely in terms of hardware and software, watching, with equal amounts of fascination and frustration, as CPU speeds and RAM capacities play leap frog with programming breakthroughs. In a technological parry and thrust that only manufacturers and retailers can truly enjoy, this year's software pushes last year's hardware to its limits, leading to next year's purchase of new equipment, in a seemingly endless spiral. The remarkably good news is that costs continue to decline while processing power goes up. The less good news is that for all of that astonishing progress, none of it is likely to mean very much to the long-range prospects of the nonprofit culture. For insight into that future, we'll have to look elsewhere than to the research and development labs of Intel and Microsoft. No one learned very much about the ultimate direction of the broadcast industry by staring at the back of a television set, after all, and it behooves us now to devote at least as much attention to the material that will be flowing through the online pipes of the next century as we lavish on those glorious pipes themselves.

The prospect of a broadband, interactive, multimedia network, integrating voice, video, and data, is indeed a tantalizing one. The potential implications for virtually every aspect of the arts—from marketing and audience development to the production, presentation, and storage of programming—are profound. Technological breakthroughs such as fiber optics and wireless transmission are bringing the information superhighway much closer to our homes. Future breakthroughs in video compression and digital signal processing are bringing a new delivery platform for the arts tantalizingly close. So, too, is High Definition

Television (HDTV) eventually coming our way, sometime around the turn of the century, according to the Federal Communications Commission.

Yet in the larger scheme of things, the changing technological landscape may appear to be the last thing arts organizations need to worry about. In comparison to the constant struggle to raise funds, or such thorny issues as cultural equity and freedom of expression, visions of a new information infrastructure in the next century may seem like eons away. The future is upon us, and the arts ignore technology at their peril.

It would be an equally grave mistake to assume that technology alone will solve the problems of the nonprofit arts, or even that the new communications technologies won't initially raise as many questions as they answer. For we are approaching a change in the cultural landscape of this country as pervasive as the advent of the broadcast media earlier this century, and with as many implications for the arts as the development of the public-private support structure for 501(c)(3) organizations. The parallels are instructive. Neither the reservation of spectrum for public broadcasting nor regulations permitting tax-deductible gifts came easily, and not, at least, without considerable public debate, policy formulation, legislation, and continued monitoring. Such effort, already well underway, will be required to ensure that the new information infrastructure will be hospitable to the nonprofit sector, including the arts.

"We recommend a public-private partnership to digitize cultural materials to make them available on the new technologies. To fulfill its potential to educate and enlighten, the information superhighway must be enriched by cultural content."

JOHN BRADEMAS, *CHAIRMAN*, PRESIDENT'S COMMITTEE ON THE ARTS AND THE HUMANITIES

Perhaps more than any other aspect of contemporary life, the various ways in which we transmit and receive a wide range of information and entertainment is undergoing a fundamental change. Both in the conversion from analog to digital, and in the gradual convergence of the telephone, publishing, entertainment, and computer industries, the communications infrastructure of the next century will differ significantly from the existing patchwork quilt of mutually exclusive technologies. If the implications of these changes for the nonprofit sector are not immediately clear, it certainly cannot be assumed that the benefits will invariably be extended to that sector.

In the absence of regulations for full, two-way connectivity, for nondiscriminatory access to video platforms, and for support for training, production, and distribution, the new technology will represent little more than another lost opportunity for the arts, and another source of formidable competition for the leisure time and disposable income of Americans. Already the World Wide Web, for all of its remarkable breadth and variety (a mixed blessing, actually, for anyone searching for a particular nugget of information amidst the mountain of data) is starting to betray the same traffic patterns as the mainstream media. Undeniably, there is a lot of work of considerable merit sprinkled throughout the Web, but much of it is a fairly well-kept secret.

In the meantime, though, a number of issues remain to be addressed, and it behooves the arts community to make its voice heard concerning the implications for nonprofit culture of a range of telecommunications issues:

ACCESS: Cultural organizations of all types and all sizes must have access to the emerging communications infrastructure. We might expect that large institutions will have the wherewithal and foresight to establish branch operations in the online world. We must make certain that smaller, community-based groups, cultural centers of color, artist-run organizations, and individual artists not affiliated with institutions are also guaranteed affordable access to advanced telecommunications services, and not simply so they can dial in to a system designed and implemented by others, but so they can play a role in shaping the new digital landscape.

Much has been written about the danger of our becoming a nation of information haves and have-nots, the current "digital divide" (26 percent of white households own computers, for example, compared to only 10 percent of Hispanic households, and 9 percent of African American households). We must see to it that the cultural community does not fall, either through political oversight or its own failure to act, into the latter category. The responsibility here is two-fold: on policy makers, to enact provisions for the encouragement and support of noncommercial programming, and on arts organizations themselves, to prepare for the time when such programming will be in demand. The Clinton administration's commitment to ensuring that "every library and classroom, every clinic and hospital" is connected to the NII by the year 2000 is a laudable one, but museums, cultural centers, and other nonprofit arts organizations should be added to the list of essential destinations on the Information Superhighway.

DIVERSITY: If the marketplace of ideas is central to American democracy, the marketplace of creativity is no less central to American culture. Yet just as the diversity of viewpoints is threatened by media agglomeration and constricted systems of communications, so is the vitality of American culture undermined by the homogenizing tendencies of the mass media and commercial entertainment. Unfortunately, the new telecommunications legislation relaxes rather than tightens restraints on the concentration of media ownership. A quick scan of the radio dial, a glance at the Nielsen ratings or the best-seller lists all suggest the creeping uniformity of conglomerate culture. It is not that diversity does not exist, for it does, in folk traditions and modern experimental forms alike, from Mexican *conjunto* to computer music, from cowboy poetry to hypertext novels. In purely economic terms—in the reality of getting those goods to market—such forms of expression are the cultural equivalent of endangered species.

The new communications infrastructure holds the potential to revitalize our culture by bringing the margins much closer to the center—avoiding the compromises inherent in commercialization—by connecting niche markets to specialized programming, building audiences in the process, and developing a culture that is artist- and audience-driven rather than strictly market-defined. Rural folk traditions might be transported to the inner city, for example, or experimental forms made available to inquisitive minds in rural settings. The new telecommunications infrastructure has the potential, in other words, to deliver the full panoply of nonprofit cultural expression to those with the curiosity and the interest to seek that material out.

But only if we plan. And only if we work collectively to circumvent corporate designs for a new electronic world of home shopping and Hollywood-on-demand that will almost certainly prove stultifying to the continued growth of a diverse American culture. A promising development in this regard is "Open Studio: The Arts Online," a $1 million initiative co-sponsored by the NEA and the Benton Foundation that will provide community access to the arts on the Internet at sites in all 50 states. "This project is about ensuring a public culture," observed Larry Kirkman, executive director of the Benton Foundation. "We must work to protect noncommercial public space in the digital age. Artists and arts institutions, schools, libraries, as well as other independent voices must be able to make their noncommercial imprint on American cultural life and values." The two components of Open Studio (www.openstudio.org) include (1) free community access to the Internet, with more than 100 public access points in arts organizations and culturally oriented community centers; and (2) training centers for Web development projects at ten sites across the country, each of which is responsible for serving as mentors to ten local cultural organizations and ten local artists, who are then deputized, so that each one must teach one more.

EQUITY: Just as new communications technologies, properly regulated and deployed, can be used to enhance the quality of work and to promote equity in the workplace, so can these technologies be used to enhance the quality of artistic production and to promote cultural equity on a variety of fronts. Smaller organizations and individual artists, in particular, stand to benefit from a system that will permit them to reach remote audiences in a manner that only major institutions and commercial entities currently enjoy. At the same time, a poorly designed system, one whose cost and control structures are not conducive to independent programming, will severely retard the growth of what could be a much more vibrant, diverse American culture.

The barriers that must be cleared are two-fold. First, nondiscriminatory access for noncommercial programming must be secured, with provisions—if such access is to mean anything—for access as well to equipment, training, and support for production and distribution costs. Second, once such access is gained, it is incumbent upon the cultural community to see that participation is extended beyond the major institutions to include smaller, community-based, culturally specific, and artist-run organizations, as well as individual artists who choose to work outside of institutional structures. Admittedly, such issues of inclusion have been the subject of much discussion in the arts community already, and their extension into areas of electronic commerce and networking will add yet another layer of complexity to an already-difficult set of issues.

CIVIC DISCOURSE: What was once an arcane topic of discussion—the extent to which the government should be involved with the arts—has become in recent years a virtual cause célèbre, generating heated discussions at all levels of the public sector. The new online world, with the full participation of the arts community, can elevate the level of the art-and-politics debate, to the mutual benefit of all concerned—art, politics, and the online world itself. For just as the new communications infrastructure will depend on a vital civic sector for its success, so will it need an equally vital civic culture, a basic appreciation of the varied contributions that the nonprofit arts make to American society, as well as an understanding of the special needs of the arts community that must be met if it is to continue to make those contributions.

The new communications technologies can serve the arts in both respects, helping arts organizations reach wider audiences, and permitting these organizations to establish a context in which the larger significance of their work, beyond the transitory pleasure they provide, can be explored. Gone are the days—if, indeed, they ever really existed—when art can be left to speak for itself, its right to public patronage unchallenged, its value to society universally acclaimed. In addition to offering their basic programs, arts organizations will increasingly need to place their work in a social context, making clear their stake in the community. Artists and arts organizations can use the new information infrastructure to clarify their mission, to engage audiences, and to expand their programming. It is not too early to prepare for the cultural changes of the 21st century. To the extent that we're headed toward a computer-mediated future (in which "computer" refers to any number of devices designed to collect, customize, and deliver data to users in a variety of settings), cultural organizations will need to "translate" their work into a variety of formats, some of which will exist solely in the online world. Artists, too, will have to deal with the mediation of their work and the effect of the computer upon personal vision and ambition.

FREEDOM OF EXPRESSION: The arts have often been a First Amendment battleground in recent years, offering both metaphorical and all-too-real opportunities for vocal minorities to attempt to regulate and constrain the thoughts and actions of others. Nor is there any reason to believe that the information superhighway will be any less susceptible to battles such as these. The Communications Decency Act debate made it all the way to the Supreme Court where First Amendement rights were affirmed. Some furture iteration will probably

These computer-generated images are part of Martina Lopez's
"Revolutions in Time" series that appeared in exhibition on the Internet
through The Light Factory (http://www.lightfactory.org).

IMAGES COURTESY THE LIGHT FACTORY

loop back through the judicial system more than once before it is ultimately decided. New technology also holds the promise for a mediation of our differences, affording us the freedom to choose from among a wide range of viewpoints, styles, and content.

Such freedom, needless to say, will not come automatically. We must design and build a system, free of proprietary bottlenecks and authoritative constraints, that will encourage the free flow of ideas, giving artists and arts organizations alike a platform for the full presentation, explication, and discussion of their works. Controversy will not disappear, either, nor should it. But an open system, one that is hospitable to a full range of cultural expression, is much less likely than the current closed system to yield the kind of ad hominem, out-of-context attacks that have proved so destructive. This is hardly a battle that arts organizations can be expected to wage successfully on their own. Again, a properly designed and regulated telecommunications system will in itself foster alliances among nonprofits, and arts organizations should be a part of that team.

PRIVACY: Both personal privacy and intellectual property rights loom large on the new telecommunications landscape, and arts organizations, as much as any other group, have a stake in both. Although publicity might come to mind before privacy in regard to the arts, the freedom of an individual to partake of any kind of programming that networked systems might offer, without fear of either censure or salesmanship, is an important one. Particularly in the light of the attacks that some groups have waged on certain kinds of artistic expression in recent years, using such terms as "blasphemy" and "obscenity" with abandon, we'll need to make certain that digital witch hunts are no more successful than their analog predecessors.

COPYRIGHT: Intellectual property rights are equally important, if less easy to codify in the new era of digital replication, as First Amendment rights. Such matters, as with so much of the regulatory structure of the NII, have yet to be settled. The arts, clearly, have special needs, too, reflecting not only their mission to provide cultural services, to mirror and interpret the world around them, to preserve and transmit certain aspects of our civilization while adapting and modifying others, but also reflecting the arts community's great potential as a major contributor to the stream of images and ideas, sounds and stories that will flow through the new telecommunications system. This is not to diminish the importance of other kinds of content, which will also add much to the richness of the new system—the contributions of educators and librarians, health-care and social-service providers, public-interest and community-development experts. While the importance of data from such sources as these is incalculable, it remains largely the province of the arts community to determine the ultimate quality of the information infrastructure.

If that new system is to rise above the lowest-common-denominator tendencies of the existing mass media, in which purely commercial interests of the marketplace far outweigh standards of critical excellence and cultural diversity, it will do so by seeing that the vast resources of the nonprofit cultural sector—the riches of our dance companies and museums, theatrical and musical ensembles, and the creativity of our individual artists—are brought to bear on the emerging telecommunications infrastructure.

As the potential producers of much of the substantive content in this new system, the cultural community has a significant stake in seeing (1) that adequate standards are established to accommodate the entire range of audio and visual material that the arts require for their full impact to be felt; (2) that the tools that will be used both to produce and distribute this material will be accessible; and (3) that training, technical assistance, and support will be available to enable those with programming potential to deliver that material to interested audiences. Anything less will result in a system that will fail to reach its full potential, a system that will shortchange both the artists and the audiences of the future. This is a lesson that the arts community must learn: the future begins now. The active participation of the arts community in staking a claim for culture on the information superhighway, in effect—both imagining the future and working for the regulations and standards that will make that vision a reality—is not simply an option anymore. It's a necessity.

SEEKING NEW SOLUTIONS

If the American Canvas forums raised more questions than they answered—questions concerning the evolving role of the arts in American society, the health of the nonprofit sector in general and its coexistence with increasingly dominant commercial forces in particular—the forum participants came up with an impressive array of answers, too. Many of these involved new, more inclusive ways of defining our cultural pursuits, admitting the validity of less formal, more pervasive and participatory forms of expression. Art is no longer just for artists, and for their specialized, discerning audiences. Rather, art has something to offer all Americans.

In the process of expanding our cultural lexicon, other American Canvas participants described a future in which the arts, writ large, would play a much more central role in the lives of our communities. No longer restricted solely to the sanctioned arenas of culture, the arts would be literally suffused throughout the civic structure, finding a home in a variety of community service and economic development activities—from youth programs and crime prevention to job training and race relations—far afield from the traditional aesthetic functions of the arts. This extended role for culture can also be seen in the many new partners that arts organizations have taken on in recent years, with school districts, parks and recreation departments, convention and visitor bureaus, chambers of commerce, and a host of social welfare agencies all serving to highlight the utilitarian aspects of the arts in contemporary society. At the American Canvas forum in his city, for example, Los Angeles City Councilman Joel Wachs spoke of the need to integrate the arts into the work of neighborhood councils, planning commissions, and similar agencies designed to serve civic and community needs. "I think we have to look at our structures for doing this," explained Wachs, describing the shared responsibility of searching for new areas in which the arts might contribute: "It's partly government, and it's partly arts institutions, and it's partly business...."

The American Canvas initiative itself was part of that exploration, a process that can be reduced, ultimately, to a search for new money, new alliances, and new ways of thinking about the arts in American society—fundraising, collaboration, and advocacy, in other words, standard themes in the nonprofit sector, to be sure, but ones that have been treated to some surprising variations in recent years, at the American Canvas forums and elsewhere.

"...THE ARTS ARE A TOOL IN THEIR NEIGHBORHOOD..."

Funding invariably looms large in discussions of the future of the arts, and the American Canvas forums proved no exception in this regard. Recognizing the strain on existing public and private sources of support, however, American Canvas participants were quick to point to potential new revenue streams, many originating outside of the traditional sources of arts support. Los Angeles Department of Cultural Affairs General Manager Aldolfo Nodal cited $3 million in federal economic development funds that are helping to build a new theater in Canoga Park. The transportation and criminal justice systems, similarly, are among a number of other areas with which the arts community might profitably develop new relations. "We need to link into all of those support mechanisms and get that support," Nodal insisted. "And the only way to do that is to build these relations...into the fabric of such basic public-sector functions as crime prevention, housing, education, and transportation." Such partnerships as these have helped Nodal's Department of Cultural Affairs budget grow in recent years, at a time when many others in the public sector have had to fight to hold onto what little they have. "I feel lucky," he explained, "because my budgets grow and we don't have the same kinds of battles.... We've been able to get across to the powers that be, and also [to] the people at large, that the arts are a tool in their neighborhood, and in their community."

They are a tool for Mary Ann Mears, the sculptor-turned-arts-activist from Baltimore (whose activism landed her a seat on the Maryland State Arts Council, in fact). A participant at the Charlotte forum, Mears offered a blueprint for integrating the arts into a number of federal programs, putting the resulting "nonarts" revenues to use at the local level. "Target HUD, Commerce, and the Small Business Administration as well as other government agencies," Mears advised, focusing on "community and economic development. Consciously model this process for replication at the state level." Both the Department of Commerce and the Small Business Administration, she believed, could do more to stress the economic benefits of the arts, while HUD should "highlight the value of the arts in their guidelines for CDBG (Community Development Block Grants) grants." These kinds of arrangements were common in the 1970s, Mears pointed out. "In Baltimore, CDBG funds helped pay for the capital expenses for three theaters (Center Stage, The Arena Players and the Baltimore Center for the Performing Arts). They were also used for public art projects.... During the Carter administration local jurisdictions were encouraged by HUD to use CDBG funds for the arts."

Baltimore has failed, on the other hand, to take advantage of a more recent federal economic development tool, the so-called "Empowerment Zones." Cities in which such zones have been established "should be encouraged to include the arts in their processes and efforts," Mears believed. "In Baltimore, which is an Empowerment Zone grant recipient, there has been no inclusion of the arts perspective. Appropriate arts connections could be job training in the arts...[and] the development of community arts facilities as community, educational, economic and physical revitalization opportunities." Artists housing can also be used as a community revitalization tool, Mears suggested. "The use of public housing subsidies for artists housing can make a project viable.... Tax credits are another tool." Mears described one such effort currently underway in Baltimore: "The Howard Street Artists Housing, which community leaders initiated and for which the city created a partnership. This is the old downtown retail district which is largely boarded up now. It is strategically located near a number of cultural institutions and the redevelopment will support those existing resources by creating a much improved environment while reclaiming an area rapidly sliding downhill."

Ellen Lovell, former director of the President's Committee on the Arts and the Humanities, shared Mears's belief that there is ample room within the federal sector for more support for the arts. "If we can have a duck stamp help pay for the Fish and Wildlife Service," she reasoned, "we can have a dedicated revenue for the National Endowment for the Arts." Lovell also pointed to promising developments at the state and local levels. "Twelve state arts councils are building private endowment funds through a variety of mechanism," she noted, "including being able to get their legislatures to pass special dedicated revenues focused on those endowments. At the local level, you have something like the Denver Scientific and Cultural District, which is a one-tenth of one percent tax that the citizens have voted now twice on themselves, that's raising $26 million a year for cultural institutions in the metropolitan area. And in Broward County, Florida, to pick one more example, they imposed a tax on video rentals and sales of CDs and tapes that's raising $2.2 million dollars a year, that's really fueling a renaissance there, especially in public art."

Speaking for the state and local level, both Jonathan Katz of the National Assembly of State Arts Agencies (NASAA) and Robert Lynch of Americans for the Arts (formerly the National Assembly of Local Arts Agencies) described a variety of new income sources for the arts. NASAA has tracked revenue-generating schemes as various as endowment income, bond issues, tax check-offs, and proceeds from lotteries, organized-crime property seizures, and vanity license plate sales, while monitoring as well the growing list of partnerships that state arts agencies have formed with other departments at the state level. Such ancillary funds, Katz notes, "can be an important component of a state's support of arts and culture. Most state arts agency leaders target supplemental funds toward specific programs or purposes, and the bulk of their agency budgets come from the state general fund." Supplementary funding, moreover, can prove to be a temporary windfall, suddenly drying up in the face of a fiscal crisis. "They should be approached cautiously," Katz adds, "when they tie the state arts agency's budget to a funding source outside the scope of the public planning process." Even with the most generous, well conceived special-purpose revenue streams, Katz warns, "supplemental funding strategies do not mitigate the need for ongoing advocacy to ensure state government's commitment to arts funding."[1]

Robert Lynch, meanwhile, pointed to local governments as perhaps the only part of the public sector in which funding for the arts continues to grow. "Local government leaders," he noted, "continue to fund the arts (more than $650 million annually) even as they face an uncertain economy and shrinking support

[1] Sarah M. Dipko, Jill Hauser-Field, and Jeffrey Love, *Supplemental Funding Strategies of State and Jurisdictional Arts Agencies* (Washington, DC: National Assembly of State Arts Agencies, 1993) iv.

PHOTO COURTESY LA ALIVE!

Two young children explore the circus arts at the LA Alive! Festival, one of hundreds
of community-based arts festivals which have special programming for children.

from the federal government…. [S]tudies show that because of the social, educational, and economic benefits provided by the arts, local leaders consistently
increase support for the arts by seven percent in the aggregate annually, often
through very innovative funding means."[2] Funds derived from those innovative
means, according to Lynch, include $36 million from property taxes in St. Louis,
which allow the major institutions to provide free admission to members of the
community; $10 million from the hotel/motel tax in San Francisco, for arts activi-
ties that increase cultural tourism; and $5 million from the gambling tax in
Deadwood, South Dakota, to support culture and preservation activities. These and
other innovative programs are highlighted in the Institute for Community
Development and the Arts's *Resource Development Handbook: Untapped Public*

---

[2] National Assembly of Local Arts Agencies, *Building America's Communities: A Compendium of Arts and
Community Development Programs* (Washington, DC: Institute for Community Development and the Arts,
1996) 4-5.

Funding for the Arts, a useful compendium of alternative funding sources in the public sector.[3]

For better or worse, though, most of the programs that Lovell, Katz, and Lynch described, novel though they may be, involve the taxing power of the state, a power that few legislatures are enthusiastic about exercising in these times of shrinking governments. (It's little wonder, then, that the slogan that carried the hotel/motel tax measure in St. Louis—"You never paid it, you never will!"— emphasized the fact that visitors rather than residents would be footing the bill.) That's one of the reasons that Delaware, in its effort to find new money for its major cultural institutions, came up with an entirely new plan.

"...THE DELAWARE MODEL..." "One thing that you never say in Delaware," laughs Peggy Amsterdam, director of the state's Division of the Arts, "is that three letter word that starts with a 't' and ends with an 'x.'" Amsterdam can afford to laugh now, having overseen the successful completion of one of the most remarkable achievements in all of cultural philanthropy—the Delaware Arts Stabilization Fund. "It was in 1987-88," Amsterdam recalls, a time when she was still the program specialist in charge of major institutions. "The TCG [Theatre Communications Group] report had just come out, about arts organizations on the edge, and we had several arts organizations who were on the edge or about to go over the edge, as it were. They were really having a hard time." Problems tend to stand out more in a state like Delaware, notes Amsterdam. "This is a very small state...everybody knows everybody, and our relationship with the arts organizations has been very close. They understand that they need to tell us things, even the bad things, so that we can help them out."

A few of the largest organizations in Delaware had come forward with rather severe economic problems, but their proposed solution—going to the state legislature for individual line items—was likely to create more problems than it solved. So the arts council organized a meeting with the state official to which the agency reports, the Secretary of State, and invited the organizations to make their case for special assistance. "The Secretary of State at the time was a very savvy polit-ical person," Amsterdam notes, "and he said, 'You know what? You can all go in

---

[3] Dian Magie, ed., *Resource Development Handbook: Untapped Public Funding for the Arts* (Washington, DC: National Association of Local Arts Agencies, 1995).

there asking for your individual money, and you…all have influential boards, and some of you are going to win and some will lose, and you're all going to look like idiots doing it. My suggestion is, put your heads together, come up with a solution to the problem, and I'll support you in what you need to do, to get you the money from the legislature that you need.'"

Ultimately, eight of Delaware's largest arts organizations—the Christina Cultural Arts Center, Delaware Art Museum, Delaware Symphony, Delaware Theatre Company, Grand Opera House, OperaDelaware, Rehoboth Art League, and Wilmington Music School—met to discuss their mutual problems and concerns, as well as their basic differences, and came up with a plan focusing on their capital needs—debt elimination, cash reserves, and facility maintenance and operation funds. These are among the less glamorous items on the fundraiser's wish list, less glamorous than arts programming and special project costs, certainly, but they are no less crucial to the overall health of an arts organization. One question remained, however, concerning the size of an endowment that would produce sufficient annual income to meet the needs of all eight organizations.

"We got them all to say what they really needed," Amsterdam explains, "and then we took a look at the numbers. We had an independent CPA come in…. We looked at everything, and determined that we needed $21.5 million to draw off enough income to give these organizations what they needed." That's a lot of money anywhere these days, but in a state the size of Delaware, whose population of 700,000 would rank fifteenth in the country if it were a city rather than a state, it's a small fortune. Undaunted, the eight organizations, now formally known as the Arts Consortium of Delaware (ArtCo), renewed their pitch to the Secretary of State, who vowed to get them exactly $5 million—$1 million a year for five years, with the balance to be made up in contributed income.

Eventually, that match was made with the help of nearly 100 private- and public-sector contributors, spearheaded by the CEOs of Dupont, Hercules, and MBNA America Bank, and including a $750,000 Challenge Grant from the Arts Endowment (the first ever in Delaware, and the largest awarded by the arts endowment in 1995). "We created a partnership that connects the social, cultural and economic development of Delaware with its business, public and foundation communities," explains Thomas Graves, co-chairman of the Grand Opera House and chairman of the endowment campaign. "This campaign was successful because each partner understood it had an equal stake in seeing that the $21.5 million was in place. We believe this statewide partnership and endowment in Delaware is unique. We could find no model anywhere across the country to follow, so representatives from the arts, business, government and foundation sat down together and designed the Delaware model."

Key to the success of that model, Amsterdam believes, is the aspect of leveraging, using the challenge concept to its full potential by creating an interlocking public-private structure of long-term commitments. "We asked the donors to make their pledges over five years," Amsterdam explains, "and to make them contingent on having the state maintain its $1 million annual contribution, so that the second year, when the state was looking at saying, 'You don't really need a million dollars, we'll give you $750,000,' we said, 'Oh no, you can't do that, because then Dupont isn't going to give us their contribution.' We had letters that said that. We really leveraged the whole thing on everybody else."

The other key to ArtCo's success, one that continues to pay dividends today, is the element of cooperation. "Not only did we bring the arts organizations together, and make them appreciate one another's problems and what they were dealing with," Amsterdam notes, "but we also brought in the foundation and the corporate community and laid the cards on the table, and they came along with us. I think that's pretty unique. We had bank presidents going with us to ask for money from other organizations. We had the three corporate leaders call groups of people in for breakfast and say, 'OK we've got a month to raise another million dollars, how are we going to do it?'"

But the Delaware model is more than a fundraising frenzy, one designed to meet its goal at all costs, with no concern for the larger implications of the effort, or for its impact on other arts institutions in the state. "One of the most important things that we did," according to Amsterdam, "was that we explained to the funders in great detail why this pledge couldn't take the place of the current operating funding that they were giving to the arts organizations. Because without those funds they'd still have to close their doors. There wouldn't be any programs." Additionally, five percent of the ArtCo funds have been set aside for smaller, nonmember organizations that may be experiencing capital needs of their own. "For the first three years," notes Amsterdam, speaking of these set-aside funds, "we left our money in the bank to grow, because we didn't really have a lot. And then last year for the first time, we gave out a little over $20,000. It was great because we had a couple of small organizations in the southern part of the state who were having some real problems, and it really made a difference. This year we're going to give out $40,000."

Beyond the funds themselves, Amsterdam cites as well a nonpecuniary benefit of the consortium effort, one that has allowed the participants to work more closely together in a variety of ways. "I never realized," says Amsterdam, "that an art museum didn't understand what a symphony did, and what their needs were and what their concerns were and what their challenges were, and vice versa…the symphony didn't know what a theater company did. It's very interesting that our community now is very tight…."

"The collaboration is really the interesting thing," she adds. "Right now, we're looking at collaborating on developing Web pages, so that we're all going into one organization for a grant that will create Web pages for all the arts organizations, and one of the local banks is looking at that as a marketing tool. The other thing that we're looking at is a cultural tourism program…and things like a 1-800 number for the arts…and a shared box-office operation. So there are efficiencies recognized because of that."

The "Delaware model," given the size of that state and the generosity of its corporate sector, might not be easy to replicate elsewhere; but its general principal—a reliance on investment income from a fixed endowment rather than a dependence on either public or private support—is worthy of consideration. Another model, more broadly conceived, is Arts Stabilization (formerly the National Arts Stabilization Fund), an organization based in New York that serves communities across the country. Established by the Ford Foundation in 1983 (with initial funding from the Ford, Rockefeller, and Andrew Mellon foundations), Arts Stabilization combines technical assistance, long-range planning, and multi-year matching grants for participating organizations within a given community. Communities served thus far (involving some 700 organizations and nearly $50 million in support from over 250 corporations, foundations, and government agencies) include Boston, Kansas City, Seattle, New York City, Baltimore, Columbus, and the state of Arizona.

Arts Stabilization programs are designed to help organizations plan now for future needs, breaking the cycle of crisis management and emergency fundraising campaigns that have long afflicted the arts. "Effective management and financial stability," former Arts Stabilization President Len Vignola has written, "can provide the optimum environment for creative artistic expression."[4] Or, as one

[4] National Arts Stabilization Fund, *Ten Years of Service to Arts Organizations* (New York: National Arts Stabilization Fund, n.d.) 17.

organizational participant in the Arts Stabilization process put it, "Sound finances make our art better."

"THE DIFFICULT ECONOMIC REALITIES OF ARTISTS' LIVES..."

Unfortunately, the only real "stabilization program" that exists for most individual artists today is a steady job, and many times even these prove to be more of a distraction to the creative process than an inspiration. "Today, the American artist is an endangered species," performance artist Guillermo Gomez-Peña has observed, "and our cultural institutions, especially the most visionary ones, have been dramatically defunded. This has caused a national conversation regarding the survival of creativity. Throughout the country, arts organizers, funders and artists are desperately seeking new models of survival." These proposed models, Gomez-Peña notes, "range from the common-sensical to the outrageous. Some colleagues truly believe that we can cross over with dignity into mass media and entertainment. And there is a precedent for this: performance artists like Laurie Anderson, Spalding Gray, and Anna Deveare Smith have been successful to different degrees. And some spoken word poets have found a niche on MTV. But these options clearly can only exist for a handful of artists."

Gomez-Peña, the recipient of a MacArthur fellowship and one of the busiest artists in the country, is part of that fortunate handful, but he expresses concern for the vast majority of artists who are forced to labor in relative obscurity. "At the moment my main worry is the survival of the next generation," he explains. "The hundreds of thousands of art students and young and emerging artists now facing a world of minimal options, not that different from any third-world country without the resources to produce and promote the arts. If they develop some computer and animation skills, they might get lucky and find a job at Disney, or a computer firm, or a CD-ROM company. But again, just a tiny percentage will get hired, and certainly not to develop their own projects."[5]

Fellowships and commissions are available, but their coverage across disciplinary and geographical boundaries is spotty at best. Especially since the demise of artist fellowships at the federal level (all but eliminated by Congress in 1996), individual artists face uncertain prospects. One encouraging prospect in this regard,

[5] Guillermo Gomez-Peña, "Arts Funding Cuts Commentary," Latino USA broadcast, 22 Mar. 1997.

however, is an effort that grew out of the ashes of individual artist support at the federal level, of which only literary fellowships remain among the 12 programs that once accepted individual applications.

"The [United States of America] needs urgently to

renew and reorganize its investment in its people....

A country whose prosperity is based on creativity,

flexibility, and openness to change needs to equip

its people accordingly."

THE *ECONOMIST*, 1993

In the fall of 1995, the steering committee of the Artists Project Regional Initiative (an NEA program, also funded by the Rockefeller Foundation and other private organizations, that provided support to well over a thousand artists in its ten years of operation before it was terminated) convened a meeting in Chicago with the National Artists Advocacy Group (a recently formed consortium of more than 20 national arts organizations) to develop "coordinated strategies for the field of artist support."[6] The themes discussed at this meeting included (1) the overall need for research, to enhance our understanding of both the condition and contributions of artists; (2) the importance of nonfinancial support, including critical recognition, technical assistance, and organizational support; (3) the need to counter societal misconceptions about art and artists; and (4) the need to build effective coalitions, both within the arts community and among the arts and other interest groups.

---

[6] NAAG members include the National Association of Artists' Organizations, the National Campaign for Freedom of Expression, Atlatl, the National Association of Latino Arts and Cultures, and the National Alliance for Media Arts and Culture. The discussion of this project is based on a report written by Anne Focke, "Financial Support for Artists: A Study of Past and Current Support, with Reflections on the Findings and Recommendations for Future Action," Dec. 1996.

Additional meetings followed, and veteran arts administrator and consultant Anne Focke was hired to conduct a study of the existing opportunities and possible future programs for the support of individual artists. Although this effort began with the assumption that a "national trust for artists" was needed, one that would offer financial support across all disciplines and in all states, it soon evolved into a more broad-based inquiry into the varied needs of artists. "Future thinking about ways to strengthen artists' economic circumstances," Focke reports, "should consider the whole range of ways that they get a living, not just narrowly designed grant programs for artists."[7]

Like many long-range planning efforts in the arts, this one began in the midst of crisis, with the elimination of most federal funding for individual artists, and with a perceived need to act quickly to find a replacement for these lost funds. But Focke reminds us that "even when the now-discontinued programs were in place and operating energetically, many artists—artists who were contributing to their neighbors and communities, to the theoretical evolution of their art forms, even to their local economies—were struggling financially. The difficult economic realities of artists' lives are not a recent phenomenon, but rather are deeply rooted. The work we do now should aim for more than simply getting back to where we were in 1990 before the recent controversies and Congressional battles. We need new perspectives to frame our move forward."[8]

In making that move forward, Focke suggests six areas of concern. Although these are of particular relevance to the needs of individual artists, they should also be of interest to the arts community more generally—individuals, institutions, and their audiences alike:

~ Information: building an inclusive database of information about programs of financial support for artists.

~ Member services: collaborating to make available for artists a range of services and benefits.

~ Advocacy: engaging in broad-reaching advocacy based on understanding artists as citizens, and aimed at improving economic conditions.

~ Communication: inspiring each other; communicating and exchanging ideas; establishing loose ties among our initiatives.

[7] Focke "Financial Support" 4.
[8] Focke "Financial Support" 5.

~ Money: creating new and strengthening existing financial mechanisms and sources.

~ Research and publishing: studying, publishing, and thinking about artists/culture and economics, and the way forces in each overlap.

However work in these several areas proceeds, Focke offers sound advice for anyone surveying the cultural landscape, regardless of whether one's primary concern is institutional or individual, public or private, or the entire nonprofit arts infrastructure itself: "I strongly suggest that we find an energy that does not rely on a sense of crisis. Running on the fuel of one crisis after another is exhausting, seems likely to foster shallow argument, and probably can't be sustained in any case. We need to base our efforts on a deeper energy with longer lasting momentum. The big things won't change quickly."[9]

"...MAYBE THERE IS A DIFFERENT WAY THAT WE CAN DO BUSINESS..."

The "big things" probably won't change at all, in fact, unless the arts community can mount more of a united campaign, one that reaches beyond the boundaries of the arts themselves into other areas of American life. The call for collaboration is nothing new, of course. Funders have been demanding it for years, arts consultants prescribe it like aspirin ("take two joint ventures and call me in the morning"), and service organizations have hosted conferences based on this theme for decades.

That advice is no less true for having been repeated so often, however, and especially as these coalition-building efforts serve to widen the circle of the non-profit culture, bringing in both new voices and new sources of support, the strategy is a sound one. It's one that funders are finding increasingly attractive, certainly, as Jorge Jackson, vice president of public affairs of GTE California, made clear at the Los Angeles forum. "From our perspective," Jackson explained, "we would rather [support] collaborative efforts where people of different backgrounds in the arts come together in the interest of a community project or a school project. We like to see the interactivity. We find that when we fund programs that are clearly desig-nated for one segment of society, that many times we build walls rather than bridges and so…what is really working for us with our limited resources are those partnership, those collaborative efforts…."

[9] Focke "Financial Support" 45.

Deena Epstein, program officer with the George Gund Foundation, agreed. Speaking at the American Canvas forum in Columbus, Epstein explained that "what we have tried to do is to work with organizations to get them to think more collaboratively, to think smarter, to work faster and better, if you will." She cited the example of a school of the arts in a Cleveland neighborhood, where private music lessons were generally beyond the means of most families. Through an arrangement with a near-by music conservatory, which provided its students as teachers, and with the local community college, which offered classroom space on Saturday mornings, the community now has a thriving program of private music lessons. Some of its graduates, in fact, are now entering the community college as music majors, and from there they will be able to enter the conservatory to complete their studies. "Those are the kinds of things that [can be done] with limited dollars," Epstein observed. "You have to begin to think smarter, to think more collaboratively, to kind of move out of the box, beyond what was your traditional way of doing business, to thinking maybe there is a different way that we can do business and look for new partners."

In the public sector, Lakin Ray Cook, executive director of the West Virginia Commission on the Arts, spoke at the Columbus forum of a collaboration that has found new partners across another kind of border entirely. "One of the most unique partnerships developed by the commission," Cook explained, "began in 1995 in partnership with the Ohio Arts Council. Ohio and West Virginia share a border on the Ohio River from Gallipolis, Ohio, to Weirton, West Virginia. Both state agencies saw the need to assist communities along the river in the development of their cultural heritage. This nine-county area in Ohio and eleven-county area in West Virginia is partially a mix of rural and recovering 'rust-belt' or heavy chemical plant and manufacturing communities. They all share the influence of the river in their heritage."

Following a series of planning meetings, the staffs of the two arts councils came up with the Ohio River Border Initiative (ORBI), supported by private, state, and federal sources, as a means of both serving the cultural needs of these communities and creating a "bridge" across the river between them. "The ORBI project is working to bring together arts and nonarts groups to define the ORBI area," Cook explains, "…geographically, culturally, and on the basis of desired outcome." The first two years of pilot grants produced a number of examples of that outcome:

~ "Talking Across the Lines"—a project of oral history, music, and stories of Bridgeport, OH, Wheeling, WV, and Steubenville, OH.

~ River Valley Children's Choir—a collaborative project involving St. Marys, WV, and Washington County, OH.

~ A local river heritage exhibition—a collaboration among the Creel Foundation of St. Marys, WV, and the Washington County and Marietta, OH, area.

~ A community band and theater program—a joint project of the Riverbend Arts Council, Middleport, OH, and Wood County, WV.

~ African-American Jubilee Festival—celebrating the heritage of Wheeling, WV, and Belmont and Martin's Ferry, OH.

Within the private sector, Ed Waterstreet, artistic director of the Deaf West Theatre Company, described at the Los Angeles forum a number of co-productions that his company has undertaken this past season, including one with the Sacramento Theatre Company, several hundred miles to the north. "The benefits are great," according to Waterstreet, "both artistically as well as from a marketing standpoint. Ultimately, 'collaboration and consolidation' will have a strengthening effect on each participating organization. As we learn from one another, we will be better equipped to fulfill our roles in the communities we serve."

In the final analysis, though, the point of collaboration within the non-profit cultural sector is more than a matter of increased efficiency, economies of scale, or even the improved community service to which Waterstreet refers. Ultimately, the strength-in-numbers approach has more to do with developing the kind of critical mass that can withstand, however imperfectly, the countervailing forces of commercial culture that threaten to overwhelm all alternatives. Theatre Communication Group's John Sullivan declares:

What we are seeing is the creation of a global market in which capital is unrestrained, and that has led to this remarkable speed-up of our lives. I believe there are things within that economic environment which one can judge healthy from an economic standpoint, but I think it has also been quite devastating on the issues of community. And so therefore I believe that a healthy not-for-profit sector is an essential antidote to the free market. I think they must go hand in hand. I think the free market itself will over the long term be far healthier if it recognizes the need for that balance. We need enclaves where ideas are not driven by capital, we need not-for-profit enclaves where ideas emerge for other purposes than the advancement of capital.

PHOTO BY NANCY PATTERSON-BOYD

Participants of all ages, shapes and sizes come together in an
impromptu dance during a Liz Lerhman Dance Exchange residency at
the Hult Center for the Performing Arts in Eugene, Oregon.

Those kinds of nonprofit enclaves, be they literary publishers or composers collectives or community cultural centers, need more than financial support (although they certainly need that, too). They also need strong advocates, in both the public and private sectors, precisely at a time when the public-interest perspective is least popular. "It's tough territory," Sullivan concedes, "because we don't have the language to talk about these things that doesn't put us in a sort of 'leftist' corner.... We have to find language that we can use in speaking to a broader audience about these issues. And that's the challenge."

"...A SIMPLE MESSAGE ABOUT CREATIVITY..."

The arts community, Ohio Arts Council Executive Director Wayne Lawson urged at the Columbus forum, must find a way to simplify and clarify its message, if it hopes to compete with the simple, straightforward message of those opposed to government support of the arts. Somehow the competing interests of institution and individual, of private freedoms and public responsibilities, of cultural ideals and legislative realities, must all be reconciled, according to Lawson, in the process of arriving at a positive message that can counter the attacks. "Let us define it," declared Lawson, "and put it on that table where we are, so we can win the same kind of battle that they are winning."

Speaking in Los Angeles, meanwhile, Aaron Paley of Community Arts Resources cautioned against adopting an adversarial stance, or one that assumes that neither the public nor their political leaders have any understanding of how important the arts really are. A more politically astute approach, Paley believed, would be an arts advocacy that demonstrates the many contributions that artists can make to their communities. For Los Angeles arts writer and consultant Romalyn Tilghman, finally, the arts need a simpler, more persuasive message that will attract a much larger following, a crusade similar in size and commitment to that of the conservation movement. "Everybody [who] has ever seen a tree," Tilghman observed, "feel[s] like they're behind conservation, that that's their cause.... [We need to] get a message which is truly simple.... I think that the message we have to take out to the American public is a simple message about creativity and about the importance [of art] in our lives, and I think people do know it in their hearts."

Tilghman's invocation of environmentalist principals is not a new one. It has been strongly suggested, by Chairman Jane Alexander and others, that what the country needs is a new citizens movement, one that will do for the cultural environment what the "green revolution" did for the natural environment. At a recent symposium in Washington on arts and business, for example, Robert L. Johnson, chairman and CEO of Black Entertainment Television, suggested that the arts community needed its own *Silent Spring*, a reference to Rachel Carson's enormously influential 1962 exposé of the looming ecological disasters that awaited the country if it did not change its ways, and which galvanized a generation of Americans in the process.[10] The roots of the environmental movement in this country, as Alexander has pointed out, extend back at least a hundred years (John Muir organized the Sierra Club in 1892, for example, and his beloved Yosemite Valley had become a state park 28 years before that), but as a model for the arts, the environmental legacy is a complex one.

---

[10] Johnson participated in "The Arts Make America Rich," a panel discussion on 11 Mar. 1997 at the Library of Congress sponsored by the National Academy of Recording Arts and Sciences, Inc., as a part of Arts Advocacy Week.

As a consciousness-raising enterprise, certainly, no one can deny the environmental movement's impact on both popular and political thought. In 1965, only 17 percent of Americans regarded the "reduction of air and water pollution" to be a national priority, according to a Gallup Poll that year; just five years later, that figure had more than tripled to 53 percent, and by the 1990s, well over 80 percent of Americans could identify themselves as "environmentalists." Rarely has a social movement taken hold of the nation's imagination so thoroughly and so swiftly. Nor have the legislative triumphs of the movement (including the Clean Air Act of 1963, the Wilderness Act of 1964, the Water Quality and Solid Waste Disposal Acts of 1965, and the National Environmental Policy Act of 1969) been trivial. And yet any number of scientific assessments of the environment reveal how little progress we've made in realizing the goals of those acts: in reversing the trend of environmental degradation, in restoring air, water, and soil to safe conditions, in developing renewable energy systems, in implementing sustainable-yield forestry.

As a model for arts advocacy, moreover, the environmental movement raises some troubling questions—concerning the depth of popular commitment, the strength and ferocity of the opposition, and the danger of placing too much emphasis on Washington—questions that should be all-too-familiar to an arts community that has run aground on these identical issues in recent years. In his thumbnail sketch of the history of environmentalism, in fact, Mark Dowie has uncovered some of the very same stress points that threaten to undermine the support structure for the arts in this country. Tracing the movement back to the "remnants of an organized conservation initiative that began a hundred years ago with great promise," and which "became the organizational infrastructure of a movement that broadened both its definition of environment and its agenda," Dowie describes a movement that is far older than organized arts advocacy. And yet both environmentalism and the nonprofit arts have experienced similar growth patterns over the past three decades. Following the initial Earth Day in 1970, Dowie observes, the movement "grew exponentially in numbers of followers, energy, skill, and financial resources. By Earth Day 1990 the American environmental movement had become a vast, incredibly wealthy complex of organizations dominated by a dozen or so large national groups centered, if not headquartered, in Washington, D.C. Together, at times in chorus, the 'nationals' (as they came to be called) crafted an agenda and pursued a strategy based on the civil authority and good faith of the federal government."

Dowie faults that top-heavy organizational arrangement and its preoccupation with Washington—"dangerously courting irrelevance," he believes—as the primary reason for environmentalism's indifferent record in recent years. "The nationals...made two other, near-fatal blunders," Dowie declares: "one was to alienate and undermine the grassroots of their own movement; the other was to misread and underestimate the fury of their antagonists." [11] Both issues—the absence of grass-roots support for the arts, and the dogged persistence of the opposition—were raised at the American Canvas forums. If there were no immediate solutions in sight, the stage was set for a more general re-evaluation of the place of the arts in American life.

"...THE CRUCIAL SIGNIFICANCE OF THE ARTS..."

Sherri Geldin, director of the Wexner Art Center, began that process at the Columbus forum:

> *Over the last decade or so arts institutions have increasingly been called upon to address and fulfill societal functions that may previously have been considered somewhat tangential to their primary purpose. Throughout the country and spanning all creative disciplines, one can cite countless examples of community collaboration and partnership in which the arts have been the principal catalyst. Arts institutions have become necessarily adept at engaging civic, cultural, educational, social service and business partners in a host of mutually beneficial endeavors. Obviously, this represents a healthy phenomenon on many levels, particularly with respect to introducing new and expanded audiences to the arts—sometimes through unexpected channels. It does seem ironic, however, that as we ever more effectively demonstrate our ability to forge synergistic links with diverse and multiple constituencies, often adding considerably to our budgetary commitments, both public and private support for arts institutions is on the decline.*

Geldin's sense of irony is understandable, reflecting a growing concern among those in the arts that as the twentieth century draws to a close, the cultural

---

[11] Mark Dowie, *Losing Ground: American Environmentalism at the Close of the Twentieth Century* (Cambridge, MA: MIT Press, 1995) xiii.

community finds itself at the mercy of a number of forces beyond its control:

~ a growing distrust of government programs and a preoccupation with eliminating the federal deficit.

~ a narrowed focus on what is perceived to be "essential" issues—including crime, drugs, the economy, education—in which the arts, if they are mentioned at all, are often viewed as peripheral.

~ Mounting social problems that demand a greater share of both public and private resources, and which have been exacerbated in recent years by the increasingly skewed distribution of wealth in this country.

None of these precludes the kind of expanded role for the arts in social, economic, and educational affairs that were repeatedly identified by American Canvas participants as crucial to the future health of the arts in this country. Nor was Geldin alone, however, in issuing the warning that we must not lose sight of the essence of the arts in our efforts to meld them into so many other activities. Or, as sculptor Audrey Flack insisted at the Rock Hill forum, we must not forget that the real value of culture is neither in its contribution to economic development nor its impact on tourism, but is rather the sheer magic of the creative process itself, a power that can affect all of us. That's the "spiritual value" of the arts, architect Ray Huff agreed, which should not be overlooked.

"Perhaps, then, it's time to reexamine and even reposition our claim on the public weal," Geldin concluded:

> It remains true that the arts can—and do—help educate the young, bolster business and economic growth, attract tourism, provide a virtually endless image bank for media and advertising, fuel social relationships, and promote civic pride. However, it seems vitally important that we equally affirm the essential and intrinsic value of the arts in their own right as the lasting creative legacy of any society and culture. As we seek to build a stronger infrastructure for the arts and culture in this country, we must do more than enumerate and elaborate on all the ways in which the arts promote community welfare and understanding. We (and our elected and appointed public officials from the highest office down) must find ways to proclaim and underscore the crucial significance of the arts as a fundamental means of creative expression that speaks to our senses, our intellect and our emotions in a way no other language can.

Just as we cannot expect the nation's educational, environmental, and social challenges to be solved by teachers, naturalists, and social workers acting on their own, nor can our artistic culture reach its full potential solely on the strength of artists and arts organizations alone. The commitment of many others is also required to hand down undiminished to those who come after us, as was handed down by those who went before, the *artistic* wealth and beauty which is ours.

THE CHALLENGE TO ACT

The "American Canvas," Ned Rifkin, director of the High Museum in Atlanta, pointed out at the final session in Washington, DC, conjures up a number of images. First, it's the empty expanse on which the painter plies his trade. In its efforts to solicit opinions from a variety of representatives, American *canvass* comes to mind, too. But Rifkin suggested yet another meaning, speaking of the canvas that's a place of battle, the ring in which wrestlers meet to grapple with one another. Rifkin's more combative version of the canvas in American Canvas is an apt one. The arts community, long accustomed to crises of one sort or another, is battling back. That its problems are largely economic, chronic, and often beyond the capacity of this beleaguered sector to solve all by itself, however, is reflected in the regularity with which doomsday pronouncements have appeared in the arts press over the years, from the first formal economics-of-the-arts studies of the 1960s—identifying the perennial "income gap" that would forever haunt the field—through the regular red-ink updates that have appeared virtually every year thereafter.

If conditions in the nonprofit arts are to improve materially, however, something more than collaborative efforts, entrepreneurial strategies, and value-added excursions into the areas of social service, education, and civic affairs will be needed. A measure of responsibility must also be borne by those beyond the arts community itself. A variety of sectors—civic, corporate, philanthropic, religious,

CALLS TO ACTION. *The following Calls to Action, which were endorsed by the full American Canvas committee on 30 January 1997, were written by the American Canvas Steering Committee as a result of the discussions that took place in the several regional forums.*

C O L U M B U S . *The American Canvas calls on civic and community leaders to join together in recognizing America's place among the great cultures of the world through artistic and cultural celebration at the turn of the century.*

L O S   A N G E L E S . *The American Canvas calls on all artists and arts organizations nationwide (commercial, non-profit and volunteer) to work together, share resources, and broaden citizen exposure to the arts in order to strengthen, revitalize and promote communities.*

S A L T   L A K E   C I T Y . *The American Canvas calls on educators, parents and artists to work together to ensure that the arts are an integral part of their education system by recognizing the unique role of the arts as a resource for engaging students and developing skills necessary to compete in the information age that will expand in the 21st century.*

R O C K   H I L L / C H A R L O T T E . *The American Canvas calls on business, civic and arts leaders to work collaboratively in designing community development plans which recognize the competitive and cultural advantages that the arts bring to the economic, social, and imaginative life of communities and their citizens.*

S A N   A N T O N I O . *The American Canvas calls on all departments of govern-*

ment (federal, state and local) to develop partnerships within government and with the private and non-profit sectors that enhance the quality of the lives of all Americans by integrating arts and cultural opportunities into their decision-making and services.

M I A M I . *The American Canvas calls on government, the private sector and arts organizations to support and develop broad-reaching policy and services that ensure greater access to the arts and cultural heritage for all Americans.*

GENERAL ACTIONS.

1. *The American Canvas calls on artists, arts organizations, civic, business and religious leaders to recognize the unique opportunities that the arts provide America's communities and take responsibility for making the arts part of developing solutions in response to community needs.*

2. *The American Canvas calls on artists and arts organizations, elected officials, business, civic, and religious leaders to expand the description of the arts to be more inclusive of the broad array of cultural activities that the American public experiences and appreciates.*

3. *The American Canvas calls on individuals who appreciate the importance of the arts to mobilize at the local, state, regional and national levels to express the value of the arts to society and to ensure an arts legacy for future generations.*

4. *The American Canvas calls on the American public and government leaders to support the vital part of government in ensuring that the arts play an increasing role in the lives and education of our citizens and the strengthening of America's communities.*

and educational, for example—need to examine their own practices as they relate to the state of American culture. If we are to create a movement, as Jane Alexander suggests, that emulates the conservation movement that began a century ago, then the circle of those who care about art must expand.

A good beginning would be to undertake a thorough and honest assessment of the arts, to answer the question raised at the start of this report: How do we measure the health of American art? Just as environmental impact studies trace the effects of our actions on the natural surroundings, so might *cultural* impact studies assess the state of the aesthetic environment. If, indeed, the nation is as concerned about the moral climate and the national spirit as it claims to be, should not the condition of American culture be factored into larger discussions of social, economic, and educational policy?

Political leaders at all levels of government, along with the electronic and print media, businesses, foundations, the clergy, and educators might want to consider, even briefly, how they can contribute to improving the climate for the arts in this country. The shoe has long been on the other foot, certainly, with artists and arts organizations being pressed into service in a broad range of social and educational ventures. Far less often have nonarts groups been called upon to examine their commitment to American culture.

The American Canvas forums ended with the creation of Calls to Action (see sidebar), broad in scope and intent, and many of the participants of American Canvas have answered those calls (see the American Canvas section of the Arts Endowment's website, arts.endow.gov). The challenges that follow—to civic and political leaders, representatives of the mass media, the entertainment industry, the corporate sector, private funders, parents, individual citizens, and communities—are a further spur to action. An arts community that fails to look critically at the social, political, and economic structures in which it operates is one that fails to perform one of its primary functions. "The very essence of the arts is to hold the mirror up to nature," Jane Alexander observed at her confirmation hearing in 1993; "the arts reflect the diversity and variety of human experience."

THE CIVIC SECTOR. The annals of American democracy are replete with attacks on the arts and culture that later seem regrettable or embarrassing (and often both), from the prohibition of theater in Puritan New England, to the outlawing of the drum in parts of the slave-holding South, to attacks on allegedly subversive artists as part of the Red Scare. Episodes such as these are far from the proudest moments in American history, and most would agree now that they represent extreme over-reaction on the part of government officials. No one expects any kind of cease-fire in the so-called culture wars, so what can be done to improve the place of the arts in the overall context of civic life?

At the state and local levels, elected and appointed officials might give more consideration to incorporating the arts in the discharge of their duties. The same kind of "percent-for-art" provision that has long applied to capital construction projects in the public sector might be implemented more broadly—not as a percentage of the budget for programs, however, but rather as a guaranteed place holder for aesthetic considerations, including testimony from suitable representatives of the cultural sector, in the planning and implementation of civic activities such as health care, education, and public safety, for example.

Sculptor Mary Ann Mears suggested at the American Canvas forum in Charlotte, this purpose can be served in the old-fashioned way, with the arts community earning recognition on its own. "There have been efforts at the federal level in the past," Mears recalled. "At one time there was a structure to review pending legislation for arts opportunities which led to highway and Amtrak public art projects, the inclusion of the arts in CETA, USIA arts programs through the State Department, and increased attention to design aesthetics in government building...."

Artists and administrators should insist on their place at the table of civic discourse and government. Rather than complain amongst ourselves about government, we should accept our responsibility and right to engage—to vote, organize, and communicate, to inform, educate and involve government at all levels about the importance of the arts in the daily lives of the citizenry and to demonstrate in concrete ways how the arts impact upon every aspect of civic life. Some artists and administrators may well blanch and say such activity distracts from the making and presentation of art, and it does. But if we wish to improve the material conditions for the arts in the civic arena, there is no choice but to become more involved citizens of our communities, our states, and our nation.

THE MASS MEDIA. "When television is bad," the chairman of the Federal Communications Commission concluded in 1961, "nothing is worse." Three-and-a-half decades later, the "vast wasteland" that Newton Minow so justifiably lamented has not realized its potential to be—at least at the margins—more substantive.[1] Given the round-the-clock programming, might there not be opportunities for quality for the "family hour," educational programs more in compliance with the Children's Television Act, and more than the agreed-upon mere three hours of educational programming every week?

Defenders of the medium will explain that the television industry only gives people what they want. Admittedly, on a strictly quantitative level, it's difficult to argue with a system that captures the attention of the average household for nearly eight hours every day, and which generates over $36 billion in annual advertising revenues. Only when we're reminded that the nation's airwaves belong to the public, and that there are public-service obligations attached to broadcast station licenses does it become clear that we can demand better.

A useful, if not very encouraging, index of the four major networks' commitment to public service was revealed recently in a survey of prime-time broadcasting, more than one-fifth of which (12.52 minutes of every hour) is now given over to advertising. The bulk of this time is devoted to paid advertising (8.24 minutes per hour on average), and another sizable chunk (4.19 minutes per hour) go to promotions of the networks' own offerings. Unpaid public service announcements amounted to a fleeting 5.28 *seconds* per hour—a 57 percent decrease over the past two years. A similar pattern, according to the American Association of Advertising Agencies and the Association of National Advertisers, is apparent at the leading cable television networks as well. Broadcasters, of course, are not required to offer free time for public service announcements; they do so as part of their promise to the FCC, and by extension to the American public, to act in the public interest in return for their licenses to use the nation's airwaves.[2] The rewards broadcasters reap from the use of those airwaves are not inconsiderable. Collectively, the four major networks took in $6.64 billion in prime-time advertising revenues alone last year.[3] Even as the time devoted to public service announcements shrinks, broadcasters

---

[1] "I invite you to sit down in front of your television set when your station goes on the air," Minow told the National Association of Broadcasters in May 1961, "...and keep your eyes glued to that set until the station signs off. I can assure you that you will observe a vast wasteland." Val Adams, "F.C.C. Head Bids TV Men Reform 'Vast Wasteland,'" *New York Times* (10 May 1961): 1, 91.

[2] Paul Farhi, "Time for a Public Service Renouncement," *Washington Post* (12 Mar. 1997): C10.

[3] Network advertising figures come from *The Meyer Report*, an advertising industry newsletter, as reported by media columnist Bill Carter in the *New York Times* 31 Mar. 1997: D7.

PHOTO BY KEN HOWARD

The cast of "Peter Grimes" is up in arms at the Opera Theatre of St. Louis.

have another opportunity to fulfill their public-interest obligations, thanks to the valuable spectrum they have been given at absolutely no charge—an extra channel for each station—to make the transition to digital broadcasting. With twice as much spectrum "real-estate" at their disposal during the transition period, the nation's broadcasters have a perfect opportunity to supplement their standard, ad-driven fare with the kind of civic, educational, and cultural programming that is so conspicuously absent today.

Changes on television will only occur through the insistence of the community, and here again, artists and administrators have a duty. Knowing our rights concerning the use of the public airwaves is crucial. As consumers and members of the civic community, artists and administrators can organize and make the media listen to their claims, and they will be heard, if the voice is strong and loud.

THE ENTERTAINMENT INDUSTRY. On the surface, at least, one cannot imagine a more natural philanthropic fit: the multibillion-dollar entertainment industry, comprising Hollywood film and television, live and recorded popular music, and mass-market publishing, offering a small fraction of its annual income to the nonprofit cultural sector, which provides so much raw material—in artistic talent, techniques, and ideas—to the commercial sector. Sadly, that match has not been made. While individuals have risen to the cause, the entertainment industry *as a whole* has not shared its wealth with its less fortunate, nonprofit brethren.

Viewed from another perspective, this lost philanthropic opportunity appears all the more regrettable. The average cost for a single Hollywood movie last year represents 75 percent of the entire grant-making budget of the National Endowment for the Arts. Promotion and advertising costs alone for that average single movie amounted to more money than all but two states devoted to the arts last year.

Or imagine if that ticket for a seat in a movie theater included the same 10 percent excise tax that a ticket for a seat on an airplane now includes: the revenues thus derived would pay for the entire NEA budget. *And* that of the National Endowment for the Humanities. *And* for all of the 56 state arts agencies. With enough money left over for two of those average movies at $59.7 million apiece. Such a tax on popular culture is an extreme long shot, needless to say, but the entertainment industry, which spent $6.8 million in PAC and soft-money contributions to federal candidates last year, can well afford to do more than it does on behalf of the nonprofit arts.[4]

Wishing will not make it so. Here individual artists and administrators have a much more difficult case of persuasion. How do we best tap into what seems to be a natural philanthropic relationship between the entertainment and nonprofit arts sectors? Access to the powers behind movies, records, CDs and the like is as limited as access to any sector of business, and in today's marketing-driven ecology of giving, it is risky to ask for donations without offering something in return. Artists and administrators will have to search for ways to meet the entertainment industry halfway—to demonstrate the attractiveness of their creative work and how it can add depth and richness to the content of commerical entertainment, how the talent pool of actors, writers, designers, and other artists is nurtured in our regional theaters, literary magazines, and other small organizations, and that public funders— like the NEA and the state arts agencies—are the "seed money" for this network, if not the major "talent scouts."

---

[4] Based on Federal Election Commission data compiled and presented by the Center for Responsive Politics in its World Wide Web site (www.crp.org/low/cashin.html).

PRIVATE FUNDERS. One of the less amusing ironies of the support of the arts in the United States is the decidedly inverse relationship between the amount of money expended by public and private patrons (in which the private sources outspend their public counterparts by a ten-to-one ratio), and the amount of scrutiny each sector receives for their efforts. A federal grant to a performance artist appearing as part of a major arts presenter's season of activities and calculated to cost some $150 in taxpayer funds generates several pages of discussion in the *Congressional Record,* while a $10 million grant for auditorium renovations, awarded to a midwestern symphony by a private foundation, escapes notice almost entirely.[5]

Pointing out this irony is *not* to wish on the private sector the kind of inquisition and guilt-by-association that public funders have had to endure, but only to put the matter in a slightly clearer perspective. For there's a public aspect to the private funds, too, exempt as they are from taxes, subject only to modest reporting requirements. Nor is this to suggest that corporate and foundation support of the arts, amounting to well over a billion dollars annually, has been haphazard. What it has been, however, is uncoordinated, based on a time-honored system of laissez-faire philanthropy that at times, appears to be more oligarchic than democratic:

~ Twenty-five foundations (or about 0.07 percent of the total in the country) provide some 40 percent of all arts funding.

~ Fifty arts organizations (or about one percent of all arts grantees) receive 32 percent of all arts funding.

~ Five states accounted for 65 percent of all arts dollars awarded.

~ Four states and the District of Columbia accounted for 55 percent of all arts dollars received.

~ Nearly one-third of all arts philanthropy in 1992 (up from one-fifth in 1989) was parceled out in grants of $1 million or more, which went to fewer than 100 arts organizations.[6]

Highlighting figures such as these should not be construed as an indictment of the philanthropic community. Indeed, they reflect, to a greater or lesser

[5] *Congressional Record,* 103rd Cong., 2nd Sess. (1994): H4891- .
[6] Nathan Weber and Loren Renz, Arts Funding: *A Report on Foundation and Corporate Trends* (New York: The Foundation Center, 1993) 11-13; Loren Renz, *Arts Funding Revisited: An Update on Foundation Trends in the 1990s* (New York: The Foundation Center, 1995) 6-12.

degree, the admittedly skewed nature of the nonprofit culture itself, with a comparatively small number of large flagship institutions, located in a handful of cities, that dominate their fields, artistically as well as financially. The point in raising these figures is to challenge private funders to adopt, where appropriate, a more balanced, coordinated, systematic approach to the funding of culture.

Consortium efforts such as Grantmakers in the Arts (which commissioned the studies that produced the figures cited above) represent, albeit in a more theoretical than practical level, the kind of coordinated approach that might one day change private philanthropy in this country into a more organized effort, capable of addressing national problems and local needs alike, by sharing information, pooling resources, and admitting more public discussion.

Until that happens, it is difficult to disagree with the conclusion drawn by a recent study of arts stabilization efforts, one of the more promising developments in private-sector arts funding in recent years. The study points out:

> *Despite the positive outcomes of many stabilization efforts and the advances in thinking around stabilization programs, pressing questions confront the field. Grantmakers have not examined these questions in a coherent way. The Arts Stabilization study found a largely ad hoc approach to the design, implementation, and evaluation of individual grantmakers' stabilization programs. In addition to a lack of communication at the policy level, the study revealed that consultants providing stabilization-related services have few opportunities to share experiences, and the intended recipients of assistance rarely are involved in program design or evaluation.* [7]

While the public side of the arts-support structure has organized itself to a fare-thee-well—some would say to a fault—with enough associations, assemblies, and confederations to fill a large hotel, private funders often appear more competitive than cooperative. Collaborative ventures with other funders are the exception rather than the rule. In these respects, then, the private sector arts supporters are

---

[7] Strategic Grantmaker Services, "Rethinking Stabilization: Strengthening Arts Organizations During Times of Change," discussion draft, May 1995.

rather like the veteran handicappers at the race track, who tend to share information only after the race has been run. In the cultural context, we're all losers in this regard, not the least those arts organizations who must devote inordinate amounts of resources to a development staff forced to enter the "philanthropy sweepstakes" every year.

CORPORATE SECTOR. The artist and the captain of industry have long been uneasy allies, the latter, even in his most generous acts of patronage, often the subject of suspicion. It's a tribute to such organizations as the Business Committee for the Arts and the Arts and Business Council that the ties between the two worlds of commerce and culture are as strong as they are, with a degree of kinship and mutual support (for the arts contribute mightily to the design and marketing of all manner of goods and services) that is unmatched anywhere else in the world.

And yet the doubts persist. After the American Canvas forum in Charlotte, Donna Porterfield, managing director of Appalshop's Roadside Theater in Whitesburg, Kentucky, described Appalshop's documentary film and theater residency activities in rural Appalachia, efforts designed to overcome some of the social, economic, and environmental problems of a region that was deemed in a recent federal study to be "beyond distress," threatening to fall off the scale of traditional economic measurements. With unemployment running as high as 70 percent in some parts of Appalachia, with a 40 percent drop-out rate among high school students and others, and an adult literacy rate that reaches only around 50 percent, this is hardly the demographic profile that is conducive to the nonprofit arts, but Appalshop has been flourishing for over two decades. "Appalshop makes documentary film and television, theater, radio, and audio recording," Porterfield explained, "on the premise that mountain communities can assume a larger measure of control over their own fate if they can gain control over the definition of their culture and the tools of cultural transmission."

Chief among the projects that Appalshop undertakes are those that highlight the stories of Appalachia: the families on Coon Branch Mountain in West Virginia who lobbied successfully for a paved road so a school bus could finally serve their community; the widow in Ary, Kentucky, who launched a state-wide campaign to end illegal strip mining; or the senior citizens of Clintwood, Virginia, who used a residency by the Roadside Theater as a means of producing storytelling and musical events with the local high school. "These projects were funded by a combination of federal, state, private foundation, and earned income from ticket sales," Porterfield writes.

Although it has been aggressively sought, corporate funding has not been a significant part of Appalshop's funding equation. Corporations prefer to fund activities in their business locations. Because their driving motivation is profit, they also view giving as a kind of advertising—they want to see a monetary return on their investment...

At the American Canvas meeting in Charlotte, I heard much talk about the wonderful projects American corporations are funding in cities across the south—as well they should. I did not hear one reference to corporate funded projects in rural areas or inner cities. Is the message that the rural and the poor have no cultural traditions worthy of support? Or is the message that only art that produces significant monetary profit for the corporate community is worthy of support?

The challenge to American business, then, is to overcome, with at least a small portion of their charitable contributions, the market imperatives that generally limit such giving to the fields and areas that make the most 'business sense.' Ideally, a consortium approach that would bring the resources of several companies to bear on a particular art form or region might be attempted.

"So often people have described the moment of death as the final breath. We are not at metaphor's funeral. Indeed, we have had the wind knocked out of us, but we are still breathing, we are in the state of inspiration."

ANNA DEVEARE SMITH

Increasingly, companies are shifting their charitable practices away from tax-deductible company-giving accounts to marketing and advertising budgets. In light of the many contributions, direct and indirect, that the arts have made to modern advertising—in sound and imagery, design and animation—that field might be the ideal place to begin building a fund for American creativity that could serve the nonprofit arts well. Even if only top 100 companies devoted only one-tenth of one percent of their advertising expenditures to this purpose, some $30 million annually would be available to our artists and arts organizations, not an insignificant amount in these times of diminished resources.

PARENTS. Perhaps the clearest indication of the enormously difficult task confronting parents today can be found in the phrase "at-risk youth." An awkward phrase at best, eventually rejected by child-welfare professionals as needlessly pejorative, it now seems simply redundant. *All* children are "at risk" in one way or another, and given the myriad educational, social, psychological, and nutritional challenges that parents must face every day, it's little wonder that something as seemingly arcane as their curatorial responsibilities are not often acknowledged.

Yet parents play a key role in introducing their children to our culture, both implicitly, in the example they set with their own viewing and listening habits, their own cultural pursuits, and intentionally, as they share the songs and stories that are a fundamental part of childhood, as they introduce children to the media, and, ideally, as they expose their children to live performances and exhibitions. For better or worse, television will provide much of the imagery of childhood, with computers playing an increasingly prominent role in that regard, and the shortcomings of these media, both real and imagined, have been well chronicled.

In addition to playing a more active role in both monitoring and sharing their children's exposure to the electronic media, parents can also work to ensure that the arts are included in their children's schools. Vartan Gregorian, the new president of the Carnegie Corporation of New York, in a recent article in *Parade* magazine, "10 Things You Can Do To Make Our Schools Better," included restoring the arts as a major element in education as one of the things parents should do, "We've made a tremendous mistake in diminishing or eliminating art, music and dance as fluff or frills," Gregorian maintains. "The arts, like sports, play a vital role in bringing students together and promoting teamwork. Athletics provide stability and a way to release energy. The arts allow children to develop creativity and imagination.... It's almost impossible to overemphasize the significance of the creative arts in education. Make sure that your own school district recognizes this."[8]

---

[8] Vartan Gregorian, "10 Things You Can Do To Make Our Schools Better," *Parade Magazine* (23 Mar. 1997): 6.

Many parents, understandably, unsure of their own knowledge of the arts, won't know how best to proceed in providing their children with a richer, more complete aesthetic environment. The public library is probably the best place to start, where a librarian can recommend reading and other material that can expand the cultural horizons of parent and child alike, while a local arts council will have a list of family arts programs in the area. The NEA, finally, recently published *imagine! Introducing Your Child to the Arts,* a collection of essays that offer advice to parents seeking to enhance their child's experience in the arts in a number of areas, from dance, theater, music, and the visual arts to the media arts, literature, folk arts, and architecture. "Parents, teachers, schools and communities invest in the future when they invest in arts education at home and in the classroom," Chairman Alexander observes in the introduction to *imagine!*

> *Encouraging free imagination and discovery through the arts prepares our children for the challenges of the next century. When we teach a child to draw, we teach him how to see. When we teach a child to play a musical instrument, we teach her how to listen. When we teach a child how to dance, we teach him how to move through life with grace. When we teach a child to read or write, we teach her how to think. When we nurture imagination, we create a better world, one child at a time.[9]*

INDIVIDUALS AND COMMUNITIES. The American Canvas forums, which brought together leaders from the arts, education, business, government, consumer organizations, civic associations, religious groups, and foundations, were designed both to examine the various roles that the arts play in community life, as well as to highlight some of the innovative ways that communities have developed in recent years to nurture and sustain their artists and arts organizations. Those strategies are outlined on the Arts Endowment's Web site at http://arts.endow.gov in the American Canvas section. More than just another professional arts conference, then, the American Canvas forums raised issues that affect all Americans, issues directly tied to the future of our society.

---

[9] National Endowment for the Arts, *imagine!: Introducing Your Child to the Arts* (Washington, DC: 1997) 11-12.

One basic premise of American Canvas concerned the need for a broad arts advocacy movement, similar to the movement that signaled a new concern for our natural resources at the turn of the last century. This new citizens' movement will seek to ensure the preservation and transmission of America's cultural legacy. While there is no single road map that all communities can follow, there are at least six areas that the American Canvas participants identified as central to the future of the arts, six clusters of challenges and opportunities around which communities can begin to organize their actions in regard to the arts:

1. **Redefining American Culture**
2. **Supporting the Nonprofit Arts**
3. **Working Together**
4. **Meeting Community Needs**
5. **Educating the Young**
6. **Entering the Information Age**

Taken together, these six areas of concern add up to a seventh, regarding our cultural legacy, which in one way or another informed all of the American Canvas discussions. Simply put: What kind of culture do we want future generations to enjoy? How can we ensure that the finest achievements of the past and present will endure in the future? And what needs to be done today to prepare our children—the audiences of tomorrow—both to appreciate and to participate in the culture of their time?

As this century draws to a close, and as the National Endowment for the Arts enters its fourth decade, the arts community finds itself at a crossroads. Faced both with shrinking resources and with increased competition for funds, it needs to re-evaluate the nature of the nonprofit arts infrastructure, to clarify and underscore its relation to other social and economic concerns, and to determine the best means of ensuring that the full range of America's cultural riches will be passed on to future generations. The larger community, beyond the nonprofit arts sector itself, must address the challenges and opportunities listed below. We need to acknowledge, in short, that our "cultural legacy" is not simply a concern for the continued health of the arts, but is in fact a primary factor in the strength and vitality of American society itself.

1.REDEFINING AMERICAN CULTURE. Again and again at the American Canvas forums, the issue of the ways in which we define the arts in America was raised. The narrow, professional, institutional definition that we've used in the past must now be replaced with a more expansive view that includes a range of activities—avocational and ethnic, participatory and popular—within its sweep. The health of America's culture depends more on active citizen involvement in the arts than on mere spectatorship, for those who participate in the arts tend to go to cultural events. Just as our fascination with spectator sports is rooted in early participation in amateur athletics, so can a larger, more committed audience for the arts be developed out of a nation of avocational singers, dancers, painters, and musicians.

The challenge is to reach out to the majority of Americans who currently have no direct involvement with the professional, nonprofit arts, to expand the nation's cultural palette to include a full range of participatory activities, without losing sight of the standards of professional excellence that still have a role in providing benchmarks of achievement. The opportunity is to build a much larger, more inclusive base of support for the arts, one that gives all Americans a stake in the preservation and transmission of our cultural legacy.

What artists and communities can do:

~ Take stock of the cultural resources that already exist, paying particular attention to those pockets of creativity—in the community center, the senior-citizen home, places of worship and the like—that might have been overlooked in previous inventories. In what ways are Americans already participating in the arts, and how can this involvement be increased?

~ Find ways to provide forums for some of the newer voices in the community. What are the barriers to access and involvement in the arts, and how can they be overcome?

~ Make an effort to balance the needs of the professional arts sector with efforts to involve citizens more directly in the arts, through a range of outreach, educational, and participatory activities. How can cultural services be delivered in the same way that other community needs—health care, education, and public safety, for example—are met?

~ Instead of simply inviting citizens to attend the arts, find new ways in which artists and arts organizations can bring art to the people, interacting with the public outside of the concert hall and museum.

2.SUPPORTING THE NONPROFIT ARTS. Much of what we know about the nonprofit arts economy—in particular the delicate balance of public and private support, earned and contributed income—is rooted in older models largely unrelated to the realities of the present, with the sharp declines in public-sector support and increased competition for private funding. The statistical basis of our knowledge is woefully thin, and what we do know about cultural production in this country is skewed heavily toward the commercial end of the spectrum, anchored by the considerable economic clout of the film, television, and recording industries.

The American Canvas forums represent a significant first step in learning more about the current status of the arts infrastructure in this country—both how (and at what costs to the human capital involved) arts organizations currently operate within their communities, and how the most successful of them have established a network of community support beyond the traditional philanthropic models. The challenge is to communicate more effectively the nature of this infrastructure to a public that is only vaguely aware of the distinction between the nonprofit and the commercial, and between arts and entertainment. The opportunity is to achieve for the arts that same mantle of indispensability that other nonprofit institutions—schools and libraries, churches and hospitals—have long enjoyed.

What artists and communities can do:

~ Assess how the local arts infrastructure has changed in recent years, and what further changes might lie ahead. What new organizations have appeared (both arts producers/presenters as well as funders)? Which of the existing institutions are struggling financially? What are the primary sources of support and how have they changed? What facilities exist for the presentation of the arts in the community, and how effectively are they shared?

~ Identify new revenue streams that might be developed in the public sector. Does a designated local arts agency exist (either private, nonprofit or public)? Does the community have a cultural plan? Is there a percent-for-art program in place? A united arts campaign? Hotel-motel tax? Convention and Visitors Bureau support?

~ Convince the business community of the importance of including cultural activities within their philanthropic programs or their advertising and marketing budgets.

~ Work with a community foundation (there are now over 400 of them across the country, devoting nearly 17 percent of their funding—more than $40 million—to the arts every year) to develop a more systematic, community-wide support structure for the arts. Determine how other

PHOTO COURTESY YELLOW BARN

Cellist Ellen Chen is set to perform at Yellow Barn, a performing
arts center in Vermont. Artists, and their relationship to the community,
are at the core of the American Canvas initiative.

foundations might be collectively approached, to begin to address arts
funding needs on a community or regional basis rather than in the standard context of head-to-head competition for funding.

~ Provide a forum in which both the economic needs of the arts, as well as
the cultural and other services that the arts can provide to a community,
can be discussed.

~ Help to open the lines of communication between the nonprofit and commercial sectors, developing the kinds of partnerships that will bolster the
nonprofit arts economy.

~ Foster a "new philanthropy" in the community, with increased emphasis
on the exchange of goods and services and less dependence on cash contributions, encouraging arts organizations to bring both their processes and
their products to a wide range of community activities.

~ Work with the local media to begin providing more substantive and inclusive coverage of the community's cultural resources.

3. WORKING TOGETHER. American Canvas participants were unanimous in their agreement that the future of the arts will depend far more on coalition-building and collaborative strategies, both within the arts community itself as well as among arts and nonarts organizations and agencies. The challenge is making that difficult transition from theory to practice, implementing and maintaining the kinds of alliances that depend on resource sharing, information exchange, and occasionally on the subordination of individual interests to the collective good. The opportunity is to derive in the nonprofit sector the same kind of economies of scale and strength in numbers that the corporate sector has used so effectively in recent years—not through "acquisitions and mergers," however, but through a shared vision and a shared commitment to serving the community.

What artists and communities can do:

~ Determine the kinds of partnerships and collaborations that will be most effective, both in meeting the cultural and other needs of the community as well as in protecting and sustaining the cultural legacy.

~ Find ways, using both public and private resources, to reward the formation of such partnerships, in a manner that genuinely benefits all participants. What can local governments do to foster alliances among arts and non-arts organizations, taking into account their differing goals, expectations, and operating procedures? What can the arts community itself do to ensure that collaborative strategies become the rule rather than the exception in organizational behavior?

~ Foster partnerships between arts and non-arts organizations in the business, political, social-service, religious, and educational sectors, taking into account the particular needs of the community. Those alliances should include municipal organizations (social services, economic development, housing, law enforcement, etc.), neighborhood/community organizations, school districts, public libraries, convention and visitors bureaus, and chambers of commerce.

~ Develop strategies to ensure that these partnerships will be sustained beyond the original activity or event that may have initiated their formation.

4. MEETING COMMUNITY NEEDS. Perhaps more than any other American Canvas theme, the contributions that the arts can make to a wide variety of civic and community needs were seen as absolutely crucial to the future health of the arts. Arts organizations and artists alike need to become more directly involved in civic and community affairs, bringing their talents to bear on a full range of municipal activities: social services, education, youth programs, urban planning, public housing, law enforcement, economic development, and parks and recreation.

The challenge is to "translate" the value of the arts into terms that will be more readily understood in the political and business sectors. The opportunity is to transform the arts in the civic context from their present status as amenities that are added once the necessities are taken care of, into one of the primary means of addressing those necessities in the first place.

What artists and communities can do:

~ Move beyond the traditional role of the arts, in their formal performance and exhibition functions, to recognize the ways in which the arts bring people together, the opportunities they afford for participation in civic life, and the many contributions they can make to municipal affairs.

~ Highlight the ways that the arts contribute significantly to the economic vitality of our cites: as a source of cultural tourism, as a stimulus of ancillary spending (on parking, meals, lodging, and the like), and as a key factor in the location decisions of companies seeking the most attractive environment for their employees.

~ Recognize the two other significant economic contributions of the arts, both as a source of employment and as a key ingredient in the development of vital job skills.

~ Assist artists and arts organizations to bring the creative process to civic affairs, helping to address the problems that all communities must confront. Make a stronger case for the inclusion of the arts in such basic civic activities as urban planning, social services, and economic development.

5. EDUCATING THE YOUNG. Education in the arts, both in developing the audience of the future as well as in shaping an electorate—and their leaders—who will recognize the values of arts to society, continues as a priority. Equally prominent, though, was a belief in the importance of the arts to education. The arts should become a basic part of the K-12 curriculum, not simply for their intrinsic value as a course of study—to help all children and young adults to interpret their world, better understand history and one another, and effectively communicate their most profound ideas—but also for their contribution to students' mastery of other basic areas of the curriculum.

For this to happen, however, a persuasive rationale for ensuring that the arts are made a basic part of a comprehensive elementary and secondary education should be promulgated (see the Arts & Education chapter). The challenge is to overcome the budgetary constraints, time pressures, and other social and political impediments that threaten to reduce the arts to mere extra-curricular activities, available to the fortunate few but beyond the reach of the vast majority of children. The opportunity is to ensure the arts' place in the classroom for all students, not as an occasional treat, but in a sequential, curriculum-based, systematic program that is on par with other core subjects. The results, at a minimum, will be a generation of students who can create and perform the arts, understand the role and importance of the arts in culture and history, and perceive and respond to the qualities of the arts.

What artists and communities can do:

~ Examine the Goals 2000 legislation and the Improving America's Schools Act and begin working to implement their recommendations for the inclusion of the arts among the core subjects in the basic K-12 curriculum.

~ Build partnerships among schools, arts organizations, and teacher-training institutes in the interest of developing and sustaining arts education.

~ Determine which local organizations are affiliated with the national organizations that are a part of the Goals 2000 Arts Education Partnership, and work with these organizations in furthering the interests of arts education locally.

~ Encourage local school boards to adopt an arts education plan that takes into account child and adolescent development and the multiple ways in which students learn.

~ Make certain that local schools have well-trained and qualified teachers of the arts as well as artists in the schools who have a command of an arts discipline and/or a deep understanding of its forms, principles and methods and its history and tradition.

~ Assess the proficiencies of students in dance, music, theater, and the visual arts, using the standards developed for the National Assessment of Educational Progress.[10]

~ Develop a network of education, arts, and cultural organizations and institutions that are committed to arts education.

---

[10] Consortium of National Arts Education Associations, *Dance, Music, Theatre, Visual Arts: What Every Young American Should Know and Be Able to Do in the Arts* (Reston, VA: Music Educators National Conference, 1994).

6.ENTERING THE INFORMATION AGE. Perhaps more than any other aspect of contemporary life, the communications landscape—the various ways in which we transmit and receive a wide range of information and entertainment—is undergoing a fundamental change. Both in the conversion from analog to digital, and in the gradual convergence of the telephone, publishing, entertainment, and computer industries, the communications infrastructure of the next century will differ significantly from the existing patchwork quilt of mutually exclusive technologies. While the implications for the nonprofit sector of all of these changes are not immediately clear, the arts are potentially well positioned to take advantage of the rapidly evolving telecommunications landscape. As the producers of vast quantities of "content," artists and arts organizations can contribute significantly to the new system. Already, the arts community has benefited from the enhanced employment prospects of the "Information Economy"—more than 80,000 new jobs in the digital arts over the past two years alone, according to industry estimates—and the future promises to be even brighter. The challenge will be in overcoming the traditional barriers that have separated the nonprofit and commercial sectors, eliminating the distribution bottlenecks that keep most nonprofit fare—in music, the media arts, and publishing especially—out of the commercial marketplace. The opportunity is that of reaching vast new audiences electronically, converting the scattered, niche markets that have traditionally supported the arts into a critical mass, and using the new information systems to attract new audiences online. Nor should the live arts experience have to suffer in this new environment. For just as Americans today who enjoy the arts on radio and television are twice as likely to attend live arts events, so should the new media prove useful as an audience-building tool.

What artists and communities can do:
- ~ Work with public libraries and public broadcasters, many of which are already involved in developing the new computer technologies, to incorporate more arts programming within their online offerings.
- ~ Form partnerships with local arts organizations to enable them to adapt more quickly to the new communications environment, joining classrooms and libraries, hospitals and clinics as key nonprofit members of the online community.
- ~ Insist that those at the forefront of developing new online enterprises—including broadcasters, cable franchises, telephone companies, and newspapers—provide room on their systems for noncommercial, public-interest

programming, including the offerings of local artists and arts organizations. The same kinds of "public spaces" that have long been the province
of the arts in the "real world," in other words, must be replicated in the
"virtual world" that is rapidly taking shape.

Just as the American Canvas Calls to Action have elicited a wide variety of
public- and private-sector initiatives, there are any number of ways that communities can respond to the challenges and opportunities listed here. If we are to build a
citizens' coalition to create and sustain a climate encouraging the arts, we each have
responsibilities. Our artists must stay engaged in community life, for everyone who
receives the benefits of society is obliged to re-pay that debt. Our country, as well,
is obliged to preserve and protect its cultural resources. As the 21st century
approaches, let us make certain that all of the varied cultural achievements of this
century are carried safely into the next, and that American artists and arts organizations, and the communities in which they reside, continue to find new ways to
mutually support one another. For this, we must take a page from the conservation
movement, organize for action, and take care of our cultural legacy.

APPENDIX A

OVERVIEW OF THE REGIONAL FORUMS

Between June and October 1996, the National Endowment for the Arts convened a nationwide initiative of regional and community forums called American Canvas. These forums brought together local and national leaders and representatives from the arts, education, business, government, consumer organizations, civic groups, religious organizations and foundations to determine the value of the arts in communities and how to identify ways to build a solid infrastructure for the arts in America's communities.

Each of the six privately-funded forums explored a different aspect of the successful integration of the arts into communities. The hosting communities were chosen for their leadership in the development of innovative strategies for supporting the arts.

As a result of the dialogue that took place at the various sites, the American Canvas Steering Committee (see Appendix B) formulated ten Calls to Action, (see "The Challenge to Act" Chapter), one relating to each of the six forum topics and four which emerged as general concerns in all six forums. These actions were reviewed and endorsed by the full Amerian Canvas committee (Appendix B), which met in Washington on 30 January 1997 to begin the search for specific ways that their organizations and sectors can work together nationwide to assist communities in ensuring an arts legacy for future generations. Actions taken by these organizations and others are being tracked on the arts endowment's Web site (arts.endow.gov).

Columbus, OHIO   JUNE 10, 1996

HOW CAN THE ARTS PROMOTE CIVIC RESPONSIBILITY AND GOOD CITIZENSHIP?

FOCUS: What Role Do the Arts Play in Community Understanding and Civic Participation?

FOCUS: What Role Do the Arts Play in Cultural Heritage and Citizen Pride?

PANELISTS:

Phyllis Brzozowska
Executive Director
City Folk/Dayton National Folk Festival

Ben Cameron
Senior Program Officer
Dayton Hudson Foundation

Richard Celeste
Former Governor of Ohio; Partner
Celeste and Sabety

Lakin Ray Cook
Executive Director
West Virginia Commission on the Arts

Vesta Daniel
Professor of Art Education
The Ohio State University

Adora Dupree
Storyteller

Deena Epstein
Program Officer
The George Gund Foundation

Peggy Zone Fisher
President
Zone Travel

Sherri Geldin
Executive Director
Wexner Center for the Arts

Robert Glidden
President
Ohio University

Rafala Green
Artist

Michael Hightower
President-elect
National Association of Counties

Wayne Lawson
Executive Director
Ohio Arts Council

Greg Lashutka
Mayor of Columbus, Ohio

Roger Mayer
President and Chief Operating Officer
Turner Entertainment Company

Barbara Nicholson
Executive Director
Martin Luther King Jr. Performing and Cultural Arts Complex

Roxanne Qualls
Mayor of Cincinnati, Ohio

Rosa Stolz
Executive Vice President
Columbus Association for the Performing Arts

E.J. Thomas
Representative
Ohio House of Representatives, House District 27

Anna White
Executive Director
Young Audiences of Indiana

Michael J. Wilson
Chair-elect
International Association of Convention & Visitors Bureaus

Jonathan York
President
Columbus Chamber of Comm.

Columbus was the first community to host an American Canvas forum and, as such, was an effective backdrop for the topic that explored issues of civic responsibility, community pride and understanding, and cultural heritage. All of these themes were mutually supportive, as one panelist, Anna White, executive director of Young Audiences of Indiana, expressed:

"If a community has a strong sense of the cultural heritage and has a shared sense of citizen pride, civic responsibility and good citizenship will follow."

Findings from the regional meeting in Columbus included that the arts:
~ Provide a link to one's heritage
~ Are a means to understand one's community and citizens
~ Give a community a sense of identity and distinctiveness
~ Promote community pride and unity
~ Inspire community revitalization (e.g., downtown reclamation, restoration, etc.)
~ Bring communities of people together (e.g., festivals, performances, community spaces)
~ Stimulate communities' economies (e.g., tourism, corporate relocation, etc.)

HOW CAN THE ARTS BUILD AND MAINTAIN THE VIABILITY OF A COMMUNITY'S SOCIAL INFRASTRUCTURE?

FOCUS: How Do the Arts Build a Positive Legacy for Children?

FOCUS: What Role Do the Arts Play in Linking Communities and Building a Solid Social Framework

FOCUS: How Do the Arts Help to Ensure Livable Communities for Tomorrow?

PANELISTS:

Inner-City Arts (June 19)

Jerome Academia
Executive Committee Chair
The Festival of Philippine Arts & Culture

Joan Boyett
Vice President for Education
The Music Center of Los Angeles

Mary Emmons
Executive Director
Children's Institute International

Jorge Jackson
Vice President of Public Affairs
GTE California

Frank Kwan
Director of Communications
Los Angeles County School District

Kendis Marcotte
Executive Director
Virginia Avenue Project

Tony Plana
Executive Director
East Los Angeles Classic Theatre

Tom Stang
Teacher
The Phoenix Academy

Lula Washington
Artistic Director & Founder
Lula Washington Dance Theatre

Ed Waterstreet
Artistic Director
Deaf West Theatre Company

Gerald Yoshitomi
Executive Director
Japanese American Cultural and Community Center

Los Angeles Central Library (June 20)

Judy Baca
Artistic Director
Social and Public Art Resource Center

David Brown
President
Art Center College of Design

Sam Kathryn Campana
Mayor of Scottsdale, Arizona

Armando Duron
Attorney
Law Offices of Armando Duron

Michael Greene
President & CEO
National Academy of Recording Arts & Sciences

Victoria Hamilton
Executive Director
San Diego Commission for Arts
and Culture

Peter Hero
Executive Director
Community Foundation of
Santa Clara County

David Jensen
Senior Program Associate
Getty Art History Information
Program

Al Jerome
President and CEO
KCET, Community Television
of Southern California

Joe Lambert
Co-Director
San Francisco Digital Media
Center

Steven Lavine
President
California Institute for the Arts

Sally Ann Law
Associate Behavioral Scientist
RAND

Gerald Margolis
Director
The Museum of Tolerance

Alan Nakagawa
Public Arts Officer
Metropolitan Transportation
Authority

Adolfo V. Nodal
General Manager
Department of Cultural Affairs,
City of Los Angeles

Aaron Paley
President
Community Arts Resources

Brad Radnitz
President
Writers Guild of America West

Bill Rauch
Artistic Director
Cornerstone Theater Company

Sandra Reuben
County Librarian
County of Los Angeles Public
Library

Mike Roos
President & CEO
LEARN

Joel Wachs
Council Member
City of Los Angeles, 2nd
District

Los Angeles was the setting for a dynamic discussion about the role of the arts in a community's social infrastructure. Forums were held at Inner-City Arts, a center whose programs use art to build bridges between cultural, socio-economic and language differences, and the Los Angeles Central Library. Set in a county that contains 88 different cities, this forum yielded an array of perspectives that touched many of the social and urban issues facing this community.

Findings from the regional meetings in Los Angeles included that the arts have a role in:

~ Linking communities and bringing people together
~ Celebrating diversity
~ Community rebuilding, reclamation and enhancement
~ Understanding one's community and residents
~ Bringing families together
~ Crime reduction and at-risk youth support services

Salt Lake City, UTAH   JULY 12, 1996

HOW CAN THE ARTS SUPPORT EDUCATION, CHILDREN, FAMILIES AND COMMUNITIES?

FOCUS: How Do the Arts Ensure Student Success and Good Schools?

FOCUS: in Which Ways Do the Arts Strengthen Family?

PANELISTS:

Diann J. Berry
Director of Art Education
Binney & Smith Inc.

Phillip K. Bimstein
Mayor, City of Springdale, Utah

Kassie Davis
Director of Public Affairs &
Communications
Marshall Field's

Michael Day
Incoming President
National Art Education
Association

Richard Deasy
Director
Goals 2000 Arts Education
Partnership

Jerry Gardner
Artist and Teacher
Utah Arts Council

Derek Gordon
Associate Managing Director
for Education
John F. Kennedy Center for the
Performing Arts

Dennis Horn
Executive Director
Kentucky Arts Council

Colleen Jennings-Roggensack
Executive Director of Public
Events
Arizona State University

Nanci Klein, Ph.D.
Director of Professional Affairs
American Psychological
Association

Mary Ann Lee
Artistic Director
Children's Dance Theatre

Grant Midgley
Member
National Legislative Council,
American Association of Retired
Persons

Chieko Okazaki
Frst Counselor
Relief Society, Church of Jesus
Christ of Latter-Day Saints

Linda Peterson
Field Director
Utah Education Association

John Schaefer
Director and Founder
Children's Photographic
Workshop

Olene Walker
Lieutenant Governor
State of Utah

Larry Williams
Chair of the Executive Board
Western States Arts Federation

Barbara Willie
President-Elect
Utah PTA

William Wilson
Director
Charles Redd Center for
Western Studies, Brigham
Young University

Salt Lake City hosted a forum that explored the ways that the arts strengthen families and education. This forum revealed how the arts are beneficial in both childhood and familial development. This forum also addressed the challenges of making the arts part of education and family.

Findings from the regional meeting in Salt Lake City included the impact of the arts on:

~ Student achievement
~ Education reform and professional development
~ Work force readiness
~ Parent-teacher-student relationships
~ Family and community unity and growth
~ Generational relationships
~ Technology
~ Children at risk

Rock Hill, S.C. & *Charlotte,* N.C.   JULY 17-18, 1996

WHAT IS THE ROLE OF THE ARTS IN COMMUNITY ECONOMIC DEVELOPMENT AND GROWTH?

ROCK HILL, SC

FOCUS: How Do the Arts Build Communities?

CHARLOTTE, NC

FOCUS: What Is the Bottom Line? The Arts as a Community Economic Resource

FOCUS: How Can Responsibility Be Taken for America's Arts Legacy?

PANELISTS:

Rock Hill (July 17)

Nathaniel A. Barber
Regional Director
Small Business Development
Center, Winthrop University

Syd Blackmarr
Director, Arts Experiment
Station; *President,* Georgia
Assembly of Community Arts
Agencies

Ben C. Boozer
Executive Director
South Carolina Downtown
Development Association

Larry L. "Butch" Brown
Mayor, City of Natchez,
Mississippi

Kathie deNobriga
Alternate
ROOTS (Regional Organiza-
tion of Theatres South)

Audrey Flack
Painter, Sculptor and Instructor
National Academy of Design,
New York

Wenonah Haire, D.M.D.
Executive Director
Catawba Cultural Preservation
Project

Ray Huff
Architect and Director
Clemson School of Architecture
Center at the College of
Charleston

Ellen Kochansky
Textile Artist; Board Member
American Crafts Council

Betty Jo Rhea
Mayor, City of Rock Hill,
South Carolina

Deborah Smith
Executive Director
Newberry Opera House
Foundation

Leo F. Twiggs
Visual Artist, Professor of Art
and Executive Director
I.P. Stanback Museum and
Planetarium, South Carolina
State College

Charlotte (July 18)

James Borders
Executive Director
Louisiana Division of the Arts

Larry L. "Butch" Brown
Mayor, City of Natchez,
Mississippi

Paul Essex, Jr.
Executive Director
Southern Growth Policies
Board, North Carolina

Audrey Flack
Painter, Sculptor and Instructor
National Academy of Design,
New York

John A. Horhn
Senator, Mississippi;
Chairman, Senate Committee
on Economic Development,
Tourism and Parks

William Ivey
Director
Country Music Foundation

Patrick McCrory
Mayor, City of Charlotte,
North Carolina

Ellen McCulloch-Lovell
Executive Director
President's Committee on the
Arts and Humanities

Mary Ann Mears
Sculptor; Member, Maryland
State Arts Council

Nancy Meier
Executive Director
Arts and Business Council, Inc.

Wanda Montgomery
Executive Director
Afro-American Cultural Center

Samuel Neill
Board Member
HandMade in America

Kathleen Pavlick
Vice President
arts and major institutions,
Chase Manhattan Bank

Patrick Phillips
President, financial products,
NationsBank Corporation;
Board Member, Charlotte
Symphony

Donna Porterfield
Managing Director
Roadside Theater, APPALSHOP

Joseph P. Riley, Jr.
Mayor, City of Charleston,
South Carolina

Randy Ross
Steering Committee Member
ArtsWire

Rosemary Scanlon
Dputy State Comptroller
City of New York

William E. Simms
President, Transamerica
Reinsurance; *Immediate Past*
Chair, Charlotte/Mecklenburg
Arts & Science Council

Kate Vogel
Glass Artist
North Carolina

Joe Wilson
Executive Director
National Council for the
Traditional Arts

Rock Hill, South Carolina, was once a rural working community dependent on the textile industry and the railroad tracks running through the center of town to bring in people and business. Like many small towns, its growth and vitality slowly subsided as more competitive urban areas emerged. Now, through the arts, it has transformed itself into one of the state's most livable communities.

Just across the state line is Charlotte, a city that has emerged as a financial center that includes the corporate headquarters of NationsBank and First Union National Bank. It is also one of the most well supported and enriched communities in regard to the arts, as William Simms, president of Transamerica Reinsurance and past chair of the Charlotte/Mecklenburg Arts & Science Council, observed:

"I'm convinced that the arts are a part of that defini-

tion of what makes a city become a rising city.... It's

that feel-good element that makes people want to be

there, makes businesses want to relocate there, en-

courages businesses to grow. And I'm convinced that

it's the absolutely essentialpart of a city's economic

strength and economic vitality."

Findings from the regional meetings in Rock Hill and Charlotte included the impact of the arts on communities, both urban and rural, in terms of the ways the arts:

~ Aid in community reclamation and reinvigoration
~ Attract businesses to communities
~ Bring revenues to the community (festivals, cultural offerings, etc.)
~ Enhance quality of life
~ Promote corporate and public support
~ Inspire citizen responsibility for ensuring an arts legacy for our communities
~ Bring artists to the table with civic and business leaders to solve community problems of all kinds

HOW CAN THE ARTS IMPROVE THE QUALITY OF LIFE IN
AMERICA'S COMMUNITIES?

FOCUS: Why Do the Arts Enrich Community Life?

FOCUS: What Advantages Do the Arts Bring to Community Planning, Design
   and Development?

PANELISTS:

Robert Bergman
Director
Cleveland Museum of Art

Sally Buchanan
President
San Antonio Conservation
Society

Sally Cain
*Secretary's Regional
Representative*
U.S. Department of Education

Tony Campbell
Minister
St. James Episcopal Church,
Houston, Texas

Mary Jessie Garza
Lead Artist
Project Bridge, San Antonio
Housing Authority

Jay Gates
Director
Dallas Museum of Art

Ricardo Hernandez
Chair
Association of American
Cultures

Sterling Houston
*Associate Director and Writer-
in-Residence*
Jump-Start Performance
Company

Ron Jensen
Former Public Works Director
Phoenix Public Art Program

Ilene Kamsler
Executive Vice President
Colorado Hotel & Lodging
Association

John Kelly
District Engineer
Texas Department of
Transportation

Gary McCaleb
Mayor, City of Abilene, Texas

Harriet Miller
*Mayor, City of Santa Barbara,
California*

Henry Moran
Executive Director
Mid-America Arts Alliance

Raymond Post
President
American Institute of Architects

George Rivera
Director
Poeh Cultural Center and
Museum

Pedro Rodriguez
Board Member
National Association of Latino
Arts and Culture

Felipe Santander
Director
Instituto Cultural Mexicano

Rod Siler
Regional Vice President and
General manager
Camberley Gunter Hotel

Garner Stoll
Planning Director
Oklahoma City Planning Dept.

Debbie Torch
Musician and Member
AFL-CIO

Rebecca Waldman
Member
International City/County
Management Association

Jeff Wentworth
Senator
State of Texas, District 25

San Antonio's Majestic Theater was the location for the fifth regional forum. It is a newly restored venue that embodied many of the themes of the day's discussions. Topics included why the arts are an important part of community life and how community planning and design are improved when the arts play a significant role.

Findings from the regional meeting in San Antonio included the role of the arts in:

~ Community revitalization and growth
~ Urban planning and design
~ Enriching community life and citizen interactions
~ Enhancing the environment of a community
~ Promoting cultural tourism
~ Making links between a community's past and present
~ Forming cultural connections between populations

HOW CAN THE ARTS ENSURE EQUITY AND ACCESS TO AMERICA'S CULTURE AND HERITAGE?

FOCUS: Equity—How Do the Arts Provide Opportunities for all Citizens and Bridge Populations?

FOCUS: Access—In Which Ways Are the Arts Available to All Citizens and How Do the Arts Serve the Needs of Various Consituencies?

FOCUS: Forms of Expression—How Do the Arts Alllow open and Responsible Exchange of Ideas?

PANELISTS:

Robyn Brooks
Founder and Director
S. Florida Theatre of the Deaf

Teresa Hollingsworth
Folklorist/Historian
Bureau of Historic Preservation

Dorothy Jenkins Fields
Founder
The Black Archives

Margot Knight
Executive Director
Idaho Commission on the Arts

Robert Lynch
President
Americans for the Arts

Fran Mainella
President
National Recreation and Parks
Association

Jan Mapou
Director
Sosyete Koukouy

Penny McPhee
*Vice President and Chief
Program Officer*
Knight Foundation

Patrick Moore
Executive Director
Estate Project for Artists with
AIDS

Juanita Moore
Executive Director
National Civil Rights Museum

Jerrold Nadler
Representative
State of New York, District 8

Mario Ernesto Sanchez
*Founder and Producing
Artistic Director*
Teatro Avante

William Strickland
Director
The Bidwell Training Center

Gene Dinizulu Tinnie
Director
African American Caribbean
CulturalArts Center

Lisa Versaci
Project Coordinator
People for the American Way

Edward Villella
Founding Artistic Director
Miami City Ballet

Pauline Winick
*Executive Vice President of
Business Operations*
Miami Heat Basketball Team

Miami served as the setting for the last of the six regional forums, where the discussion explored the many ways that the arts promote equity and access for Americans of all backgrounds. The region's diverse geography and cultural resources informed the day's discussion.

Findings from the regional meeting in Miami included how the arts:

~ Bridge populations
~ Offer a link between cultures and ideas
~ Serve as a vehicle of expression
~ Provide a universal form of communication
~ Connect various sectors and constituencies
~ Touch communities both rural and urban

APPENDIX B

Lee Kessler
Executive Director
American Arts Alliance
WASHINGTON, D.C.

Adrian King
Director of Arts and Cultural Programs
Coca-Cola Foundation
ATLANTA, GA

Louis LeRoy
Executive Director
The Association of American Cultures
SAN ANTONIO, TX

Abel Lopez
Board Member
Association of American Cultures
SAN ANTONIO, TX

Ellen Lovell
Executive Director
President's Committee on the Arts & Humanities
WASHINGTON, D.C.

Laura Loyacono
Program Manager
National Conference of State Legislatures
DENVER, CO

Robert Lynch
Executive Director
National Assembly of Local Arts Agencies
WASHINGTON, D.C.

John Mahlmann
Executive Director
Music Educators National Conference
RESTON, VA

Tom McClimon
Managing Director
U.S. Conference of Mayors
WASHINGTON. D.C.

Penny McPhee
Director of Arts and Culture Programs, Knight Foundation;
President, Grantmakers in the Arts
MIAMI, FL

Sara Melendez
President
Independent Sector
WASHINGTON, D.C.

Leo O'Donovan
President
Georgetown University
WASHINGTON, D.C.

Arnold Packer
Senior Fellow
Johns Hopkins University
BALTIMORE, MD

Jorge Perez
President
Related Companies of Florida
MIAMI, FL

Terry Peterson
Counselor to the Secretary of Education
US Department of Education
WASHINGTON, D.C.

Dorothy Ridings
Chief Executive Officer
Council on Foundations
WASHINGTON, D.C.

Dean Rodenbough
Director of Corporate Affairs
Binney & Smith
EASTON, PA

Pedro Rodriguez
Executive Director
National Association of Latino Arts & Culture
SAN ANTONIO, TX

James Sitter
Executive Director
Council of Literary Magazines and Presses/Literary Network
NEW YORK

Kennedy Smith
Director
Main Street Program
National Main Street Center
WASHINGTON, D.C.

William Strickland
Bidwell Training Center
PITTSBURGH, PA

John Thorpe
Managing Director
Network of Cultural Centers of Color
NEW YORK, NY

Lisa Thorson
Musician
NEWTON, CT

Robin Tryloff
Executive Director
Sara Lee Foundation
CHICAGO, IL

Ann Walker
National Association of
Elementary School Principals
ALEXANDRIA, VA

Brian Zucker
President
Human Capital Research
CHICAGO, IL

Larry Wilker
President
The John F. Kennedy Center
WASHINGTON, D.C.

AMERICAN CANVAS FINAL MEETING

WASHINGTON, D.C. - 30 JANUARY 1997

ATTENDEES:

Madeleine Wing Adler
President
West Chester University
WEST CHESTER, PA

Ronald Altoon
Partner
Altoon & Porter Architects
LOS ANGELES, CA

Gordon Ambach
Executive Director
Council of Chief State School
Officers
WASHINGTON, D.C.

Roberto Bedoya
Executive Director
National Association of Artists'
Organizations
WASHINGTON, D.C.

Richard Bell
National Executive Director
Young Audiences
NEW YORK, NY

Mamie Bittner
Director, Legislative &
Public Affairs
Institute of Museum & Library
Services
WASHINGTON, D.C.

Edward J. Black
Computer & Communications
Industry Assn.
WASHINGTON, D.C.

Donald Borut
Executive Director
National League of Cities
WASHINGTON, D.C.

Julianne Boyd
President
Society of Stage Directors &
Choreographers
NEW YORK, NY

Carol Brown
Chair
National Assembly of State
Arts Agencies
PITTSBURGH, PA

J. Carter Brown
Director Emeritus
National Gallery of Art
WASHINGTON, D.C.

Robert Butler
Vice President
Directors Guild of America
LOS ANGELES, CA

Rev. Tony Campbell
St. James Episcopal Church
HOUSTON, TX

Michael Day
President-Elect
National Art Education
Association
Brigham Young University
PROVO, UT

Richard Deasy
Director
Goals 2000 Arts Education
Partnership
WASHINGTON, D.C.

Anita Difanis
Director,
Government Affairs,
Association of Art Museum
Directors
NEW YORK, NY

Deena Epstein
Program Officer
The George Gund Foundation
Cleveland, OH

Andy Finch
American Association of
Museums
Washington, D.C.

Jean Firstenberg
Director
American Film Institute
LOS ANGELES, CA

James Fitzpatrick
Arnold and Porter
WASHINGTON, D.C.

Stephanie French
Vice President, Corporate
Affairs
Philip Morris Companies, Inc.
NEW YORK, NY

Barbara Funk
Director, Arts & Culture
Division
Maryland National Capital
Parks & Planning Commission
RIVERDALE, MD

Ed Gero
Actor
Bethesda, MD

Marion Godfrey
The Pew Charitable Trusts
PHILADELPHIA, PA

Don Greene
President
Coca-Cola Foundation
ATLANTA, GA

James Hake
Principal/Chairman
Access Media/NII Awards
SANTA MONICA, CA

Donald Harris
Dean, College of Arts
Ohio State University
COLUMBUS, OH

Michael Hightower
President-Elect
National Association of Counties
ATLANTA, GA

Dianne James
Director, National Operations
American Guild of Musical
Artists
NEW YORK, NY

Colleen Jennings-Roggensack
Executive Director, Public Affairs
Arizona State University
TEMPE, AZ

James Earl Jones
Actor
LOS ANGELES, CA

Alexander Julian
Designer
RIDGEFIELD, CT

Jonathan Katz
Executive Director
National Assembly of State
Arts Agencies
WASHINGTON, D.C.

Lee Kessler
Executive Director
American Arts Alliance
WASHINGTON, D.C.

Adrian King
Director of Arts and Cultural
Programs
Coca-Cola Foundation
ATLANTA, GA

Bill Lacy
President
SUNY Purchase
PURCHASE, NY

Fred Lazarus
President
Maryland Institute, College
of Art
BALTIMORE, MD

Donni LeBoeuf
Office of Juvenile Justice &
Delinquency Prevention
U.S. Department of Justice
WASHINGTON, D.C.

Tom Lee
Vice President
American Federation of
Musicians
WASHINGTON, D.C.

Robert Lynch
Executive Director
Americans for The Arts
WASHINGTON, D.C.

Daniel Mayer
Former Executive Director
Volunteer Lawyers for the Arts
NEW YORK, NY

Mary Ann Mears
Sculptor; Member
Maryland State Arts Council
BALTIMORE, MD

David R. Mercer
National Executive Director
YMCA
CHICAGO, IL

Forest Montgomery
Legal Counsel
National Association of
Evangelicals
WASHINGTON, D.C.

Arnold Packer
Senior Fellow
Johns Hopkins University
BALTIMORE, MD

Jorge Perez
President
Related Companies of Florida
MIAMI, FL

Terry Peterson
*Counselor to the Secretary of
Education*
US Department of Education
WASHINGTON, D.C.

David Pierce
President
American Assn of Community
Colleges
WASHINGTON, D.C.

Alfonso Pollard
National Legislative Director
American Federation of
Musicians
WASHINGTON, D.C.

Ned Rifkin
Director
High Museum
ATLANTA, GA

Honorable Richard S. Riley
Secretary
United States Department of
Education
WASHINGTON, D.C.

Shirley Ririe
Artistic Co-Director
Ririe Woodbury Dance
Company
SALT LAKE CITY, UT

Verdery Roosevelt
Dance/USA
WASHINGTON, D.C.

Harriet Sanford
Chair
National Assembly of Local
Arts Agencies
ATLANTA, GA

Richard Sauer
President & CEO
National 4-H Council
CHEVY CHASE, MD

Mark Schuster
*Professor of Urban Studies
and Planning*
Massachusetts Institute of
Technology
CAMBRIDGE, MA

Amy Schwartzman
Executive Director
Volunteer Lawyers for the Arts
NEW YORK, NY

Carole Shields
President
People for the American Way
WASHINGTON, D.C.

Mary Somerville
President
American Library Association
MIAMI, FL

John Sparks
Director of Government Affairs
American Symphony
Orchestra League
WASHINGTON, D.C.

Gary Steuer
Arts & Business Council, Inc.
NEW YORK, NY

John Sullivan
Executive Director
Theatre Communications Group
NEW YORK, NY

Deborah Takakjian
Director, Board of Directors
Creative Coalition
NEW YORK, NY

Sarah Tambucci
President
National Art Education
Association
PITTSBURGH, PA

Dory Teipel
Washington Liaison
Binney & Smith, Inc.
WASHINGTON, D.C.

John Thorpe
Managing Director
Network of Cultural Centers
of Color
NEW YORK, NY

Honorable Joel Wachs
Los Angeles City Council
LOS ANGELES, CA

Laura Young
Director of Public Affairs
OPERA America
WASHINGTON, D.C.

Brian Zucker
President
Human Capital Research
CHICAGO, IL

ACKNOWLEDGMENTS

The American Canvas has been made possible through the
generous support of the following organizations:

Binney & Smith Inc.
The Coca-Cola Foundation
The J. Paul Getty Trust
The Sara Lee Foundation
The George Gund Foundation
Anonymous

We wish particularly to thank
the following organizations for their support:

IN COLUMBUS

Greater Columbus Arts Council
Ohio Arts Council
The Columbus Association for the Performing Arts
Continental Office Furniture
Arts Education 672 Graduate Student Volunteers, Ohio State University
City of Columbus Recreation and Parks Department
S.O.S. Productions

IN LOS ANGELES
California Arts Council
California Confederation of the Arts
The San Francisco Foundation
ARCO
Department of Cultural Affairs, City of Los Angeles
The HeART Project
Inner-City Arts

Los Angeles Junior Chamber of Commerce
Los Angeles County Music and Performing Arts Commission
Los Angeles Public Library's Central Library
Museum of Contemporary Art
GTE California
Xiomara

IN SALT LAKE CITY

Culinary Crafts
Salt Lake City Arts Council
Salt Lake City Corporation
Salt Lake County
Salt Palace Convention Center/Spectacor Management
State of Utah
Utah Arts Council
Utah Cultural Alliance

IN ROCK HILL

City of Rock Hill
Rock Hill Arts Councils
South Carolina Arts Commission

IN CHARLOTTE

First Union National Bank
NationsBank Corporation
Transamerica Reinsurance
The North Carolina Arts Council
The North Carolina Blumenthal Performing Arts Center
The Arts & Science Council, Charlotte/Mecklenburg

IN SAN ANTONIO

City of San Antonio Department of Arts & Cultural Affairs
San Antonio Convention & Visitors Bureau

Acknowledgments

Texas Commission on the Arts
ArtPace, a Foundation for Contemporary Art
SBC Inc.
The Majestic Theatre and the production of Kiss of the Spider Woman

IN MIAMI

Metro-Dade Board of County Commissioners
and the Metro-Dade Cultural Affairs Council
Florida Department of State Division of Cultural Affairs
and the Florida Arts Council
Jorge Perez

The American Canvas forums were organized through Pacific Visions Corporation under the leadership of Val Marmillion. We are grateful for their hard work and dedication.

Thank you as well to all staff involved in the project, particularly Scott Shanklin-Peterson, Olive Mosier, Alexander Crary, Ana Steele, Diane Matarazza, and Cherie Simon.

Special thanks to the writer of the bulk of this report, Gary O. Larson, and to all of the participants.

Published by: the Office of Policy, Research and Technology in conjunction with the Office of Communications, National Endowment for the Arts.

Keith Donohue
Publications Director

Designed by : Lomangino Studio, Washington, DC.

Printed with donated funds.

For more information about American Canvas or the National Endowment for the Arts, visit our web site at http://arts.endow.gov or contact:

Office of Public Information
National Endowment for the Arts
1100 Pennsylvania Avenue, NW
Washington, DC 20506
202/682-5400